CO-TEACH!

A Handbook for Creating and Sustaining Effective Classroom Partnerships in Inclusive Schools

Marilyn Friend

1st printing: March 2007
2nd printing: July 2007
3rd printing: August 2007
4th printing: February 2008
5th printing: June 2008
6th printing: October 2008
7th printing: April 2009

Friend, Marilyn
Co-Teach! A Handbook for Creating and Sustaining Effective Classroom Partnerships in Inclusive Schools

ISBN 978-0-9778503-0-3

Dedication

This book is dedicated to all the teachers in today's schools who

- *Deeply care about each of their students and believe every one of them can learn*
- *Work hard every day in spite of more challenges than parents, the public, or legislators can ever imagine*
- *Constantly seek new knowledge and skills to help them become even better professionals*
- *Collaborate in the belief that the results of their shared efforts are greater than the outcomes of a teacher working alone*
- *Keep a sense of humor, even when things aren't funny*
- *Know that every successful adult is evidence of their dedication.*

Thank you for all you do on behalf of your students and their families. I hope you find co-teaching is a way to help you accomplish the dream of offering all students the education that will enable them to reach their true potential.

CONTENTS

Preface

In the mid-1980s hardly anyone was discussing co-teaching as a strategy for educating students with disabilities. Two decades later, it is a focus of attention in many journals, teacher blogs, and professional organizations. Information about co-teaching gradually has become more available, but what has been missing is a teacher-friendly handbook that captures both the concepts critical for understanding co-teaching and the real-life practices and examples that can be immediately helpful. I wrote **Co-Teach! A Handbook for Creating and Sustaining Effective Classroom Partnerships in Inclusive Schools** to meet that need. This handbook is based on more than 20 years of working with school professionals and parents, and the idea for it came from the questions that I've heard from them as well as my university students. I sincerely hope that you find it answers some of the questions that you have.

Chapters 1 and 2 overview key concepts and the rationale for co-teaching. I am firmly convinced that co-teaching is far more successful if educators understand what it is and what it isn't and the reason why it is rapidly growing as a special education service delivery option. Chapter 3 outlines six co-teaching approaches, variations of them, and factors to consider in selecting them. Chapters 4 and 5 address many important issues that relate to classroom practices, such as teachers' partnerships, classroom management, and instruction, as well as the logistical elements of co-teaching, including planning time and scheduling. Chapter 6 is an opportunity to unite all the other information—it provides a step-by-step approach to creating and sustaining co-teaching programs.

One of the most common comments I hear from teachers is that administrators need to support co-teaching programs, and so Chapter 7 was included just for administrators and contains key information and suggestions for them. Finally, in Chapter 8, some of the specific questions and concerns that I hear from educators across the country, ones that may span several topics, are listed and suggestions for addressing them provided.

Best of luck in your own co-teaching efforts. I look forward to hearing about your success and to seeing the positive outcomes that you make in the lives of students with disabilities.

Acknowledgements

My husband deserves a medal for his patience as I work on projects such as this handbook. As I travel across the country, people often ask how I can possibly do the everything that I love doing—speaking to groups, observing in classrooms, consulting, working as a faculty member, and writing books. The answer is simple: It's because Bruce Brandon, my soul mate and chief cheerleader, makes it possible. He has contributed ideas, proofread chapters, cooked many meals, rescued me from travel dilemmas, and said again, "I'll help you—any way I can." How fortunate I am to have such a caring husband.

Right after Bruce, I owe a huge debt of thanks to Sonia Martin, administrative secretary for the Department of Specialized Education Services at the University of North Carolina at Greensboro. This project was one for the weekends and holidays, and Sonia—as always—persevered to see it through to completion. Her wonderful technical skills, diligence, and ability to see humor in even the toughest challenges of producing a book are invaluable. Her answer to any dilemma is, "It'll be alright. I'll just figure it out." And she always does. I'm privileged to know and work with her.

I also want to thank DeAnna Hurley-Chamberlain. As a doctoral student, DeAnna is very interested in co-teaching. She carefully edited each of the chapters in this handbook, catching the instances where my fingers were typing faster than my brain was thinking, asking great questions about content to include, and checking references. Her meticulous attention to detail made it possible to produce **Co-Teach!** However, the end responsibility for the accuracy of the information in the handbook, though, remains mine.

Finally, thanks are offered to all of the professionals across the country who have become friends as we have worked together. It is your stories, dilemmas and solutions to them, and optimism that demonstrate the potential of co-teaching, and every idea and example in this handbook came from you or the professionals in your schools. I hope you find this compendium of concepts and practices helpful.

Chapter 1
Key Concepts for Understanding Co-Teaching

● ● ● ● ● ●

Coming together is a beginning, keeping together is progress,
working together is success.

- Henry Ford

Chapter Objectives

1. Describe what co-teaching is and is not.

2. Explain how co-teaching is related to other terms used in education and special education—collaboration, inclusion, and team teaching.

3. Relate co-teaching to the supports that paraprofessionals may provide.

4. Outline components that have been identified through research as integral to co-teaching.

School professionals have complex and demanding responsibilities. Whether you are a general or special education teacher, a bilingual educator, a reading or math specialist, a speech-language therapist, or an administrator, you are expected to ensure that all students reach academic standards that are rising each year. Your task is complicated by students' increasingly diverse needs. You are charged with challenging learners who are gifted and talented, improving the achievement of struggling pupils, addressing the individualized goals of children who have disabilities or other special needs, and, at the same time, reaching those students who do not command extraordinary attention. And you are doing all of this at a time when educators often are criticized in the popular press and when some parents and community members are asking you to do more and more—with few additional resources.

Faced alone, the challenges of being a twenty-first century educator can, at times, seem insurmountable. Joining with colleagues, though, presents opportunities that otherwise would not be possible. And that is the basis for this book. Co-teaching—a professional classroom partnership—enables educators to more readily determine what students need, to deliver instruction and assess student learning more efficiently, and to tailor learning activities to the exceptional needs that some students have. At the same time, co-teaching provides professionals with a sense of support, that is, the knowledge that ensuring students reach their educational goals is not a responsibility that has to be undertaken in isolation.

Are you thinking of co-teaching in the near future? Already co-teaching and refining your practice? Responsible for creating and evaluating a co-teaching program in a school or district? Just as professionals implementing a new remedial reading program or science curriculum receive training so that they implement the program the way it was intended, so, too, do those working with co-teaching need a specific set of knowledge and skills. This is particularly true since the majority of teachers and other educators learned little or nothing in their own professional preparation about working in the classroom with a colleague. The goal of this book is to provide that knowledge and those skills. The information included is based on the rapidly accumulating professional literature on this topic (for example, Dieker & Murawski, 2003; Friend, 2007; Friend & Hurley-Chamberlain, 2007; Magiera, Smith, Zigmond, & Gebaner, 2005; Mastropieri, Scruggs, Graetz, Norland, Gardizi, & McDuffie, 2005; Pardini, 2006), but it also is based on my own work over the past 20 years assisting educators to implement co-teaching in elementary, middle, and high schools in urban, suburban, and rural districts. This book is the result of the innumerable conversations with teachers and administrators— some enthusiastic and some discouraged—about the power of co-teaching and the problems that sometimes occur in implementing it. It is informed by hundreds of observations in classrooms where professionals are closely working together or struggling to find appropriate roles. And it is based on my own firm belief that although nothing can be the panacea for all of the challenges now faced by school professionals, co-teaching can significantly and positively assist educators to reach their most cherished goal— helping their students to truly reach their potential.

What Co-Teaching Is

Successful co-teaching begins with understanding what it is. Here are the essential elements of co-teaching.

Co-Teaching is an Option for Providing Special Services

Many models exist for offering special services in schools. Some students are supported when a specialist consults with a general education teacher, as might happen when a psychologist offers suggestions to a teacher for responding to disruptive student behavior. Other students leave the classroom to receive specialized instruction, as is the case when students with disabilities go to a resource room for remediation or tutoring, or students receive speech and language therapy in a small group. Yet other students spend most if not all of their instructional day in a special education setting, usually students with significant disabilities for whom a carefully structured environment with highly specialized supports is necessary. A few students even receive services in separate schools.

Co-teaching is similar to these other options in that it is a way students receive their special services. However, it is also unique. First, the other service options for students with disabilities are outlined in federal special education legislation and have existed for many years in public schools. Co-teaching is not listed like the other options, and it is relatively recent, an option that has evolved in schools because of a need for ways to educate students with disabilities in general education settings. Second, the other service models tend to be based on an assumption that the more intense a student's needs, the more time is needed in a separate setting. Co-teaching is not based on this premise. That is, co-teaching sometimes is used as a means for students with relatively mild special needs to receive special education services, but it also can be the means through which students with significant disabilities are supported in school. How decisions about the appropriateness of co-teaching for particular students are made is a topic addressed in Chapter 5 and Chapter 8.

Professionally Licensed Educators Implement Co-Teaching

The participants in co-teaching depend on the services to be offered and the individuals who are assigned to partner in classrooms. General education teachers, of course, are the first participants. However, they may co-teach with special education teachers, reading specialists, or teachers of English language learners (ELLs). Speech-language therapists may co-teach, as may counselors, psychologists, occupational therapists, or other professionals. The key is that the co-teachers are peers in terms of licensure and employment status. That is, they truly are colleagues who jointly make instructional decisions and share responsibility and accountability.

The individuals left out of this definition of co-teaching are paraprofessionals. Although these educators play critical roles in general education classrooms, their responsibilities are somewhat different. Appropriate roles for paraprofessionals are addressed later in this chapter.

Participating Educators Share Instructional and Related Responsibilities

Have you ever heard co-teaching referred to as a professional marriage? In many ways (but not all), this metaphor is apt—co-teachers lead a classroom family, jointly establish their own culture, and address the challenges that may arise. They share successes and together solve problems that occur. However, co-teaching marriages are not all alike. Consider these two situations:

- In the first classroom, the marriage might seem like a caricature from the 1950s or 1960s...a professional version of an episode of *I Love Lucy, Leave It to Beaver,* or *Father Knows Best.* The general education teacher clearly plays the role of dad, delivering the primary instruction, setting the classroom expectations, and taking full responsibility for ensuring that students are prepared for high stakes testing. The special educator or specialist takes on the role of mom. This person—even if a strong professional—tends to be rather passive in the classroom, quietly redirecting students who are off-task and assisting students who did not understand the instruction that was delivered. Mom may believe that her role is to be a helper. If she believes that she should do more, she may feel like she does not have permission to proactively participate in classroom instructional and management decisions. That is, in this classroom, few conversations have occurred about professional roles; the teachers mostly are assuming traditional responsibilities—one teaching the overall group, the other ensuring that individual students receive remedial or other needed support.

- In the second classroom, the marriage is one from the twenty-first century. Roles and responsibilities are openly discussed and far fewer assumptions are made about the contributions that each educator should make. The special education teacher sometimes leads the science lab while the general educator ensures that all students are following the directions correctly. Sometimes the teachers divide the class in half and each one leads the same discussion so that all students have more opportunity to participate. However, the special education teacher also sometimes works with struggling learners who are greatly helped by a careful re-teaching of the material or additional practice applying core skills. These teachers blend traditional and non-traditional roles and responsibilities. They constantly are on the alert to find new ways to combine their strengths to improve all students' learning.

Which type of marriage do you think is most likely to foster student success? It is the latter, of course. However, the first type of professional marriage is all too common. For co-teaching to have enough impact to improve outcomes for students, both teachers must have a commitment to the entire instructional process and actively contribute to helping all students reach their potential. Effective co-teaching relies on setting aside assumptions and engaging in an ongoing discussion of how to engage both professionals in the process of teaching and learning.

All Students are Full Members of the Class Where Co-Teaching Occurs

Do you or your colleagues divide students as you speak, referring to "my students" or "your students?" Whenever this occurs, you are reinforcing an old system, one that explicitly or implicitly communicates that students with disabilities are the responsibility of special educators, not general educators. It is crucial to remember that special education was designed to be *in addition to*, not *in lieu of*, general education. And so general education teachers are charged with teaching every student in the class, including those with disabilities or other special needs, and they are as accountable for their learning as they are for the learning of their other students. Co-teaching tends to bring issues such as this to the surface; how ownership of students is discussed and addressed can have a significant impact on co-teaching success. Co-teaching is very much about *our* students.

Co-Teaching Occurs Primarily in a Single Shared Classroom

An assumption of co-teaching is that most instruction occurs with two educators working in the same physical space. This arrangement permits the educators to group and re-group students, draw on each other's expertise and energy, and revise and refine instruction as necessary. However, in some schools an informal agreement exists that when instruction seems difficult for students with disabilities or other special needs, those students and "their" teacher should leave the classroom. If this occurs only occasionally it probably is not a problem, but if students leave the classroom several times each week, two concerns arise. The first is that this may affect what is written on a student's individualized education program in terms of time that is being spent in a general education setting and access to curriculum. For example, in a middle school with 85-minute block periods, two teachers decide that the students with disabilities should leave the class each day after 40 minutes. If the IEP indicates that the student is supposed to be in the general education class, the arrangement is a significant violation of the IEP. In addition, if this occurs in a core academic class and the special education teacher is not highly qualified in that area, the student may not be receiving the access to curriculum promised in current federal law.

One other dilemma should be mentioned. If students with disabilities need some separate instruction, they certainly should receive it, and this should be reflected on the IEP. However, when this practice occurs, teachers sometimes have additional students leave the classroom. If the middle school teachers described above decided that two other struggling learners—who do not have IEPs— also should leave for the remedial instruction, they are violating those students' rights. If the students have not been determined to be eligible for special education, they should not leave general education to receive what could be construed as special education. This generally is true even if parents support the practice because federal and state laws clearly mandate a detailed, multidisciplinary assessment process and a team determination of eligibility and services for any student to receive special education.

A few exceptions to these guidelines may exist based on state policies or local programs (and you should check with the appropriate administrator about this). Also, splitting students occasionally to accomplish an instructional purpose is appropriate (for example, having some students in the media center working on computers while others stay in the class to work on an assignment and then switching the groups the next day). In general, though, a fundamental question needs to be raised: If the aim in today's schools is to meet student needs in general education, why not have as the most common pattern keeping students there and providing support in that setting? Any service offered there is available to all students and gives the teachers many more options for meeting all students' needs.

The Focus of Co-Teaching is Access to the Curriculum

The expectations set by the *No Child Left Behind Act* (NCLB) clarify that students with disabilities generally should be learning the same curriculum as all students. Even for students taking alternate assessments, the goal is for there to be functional touch points with the general curriculum as might happen when a student with a significant intellectual disability learned just the vocabulary about safety related to electricity while other students learned detailed concepts and vocabulary about electricity. The essential consideration is that co-teaching should not, in this day and age, ever be treated primarily or exclusively as a means for socialization.

Although working on social skills might be a specific and very appropriate reason for a student with a disability to be in a co-taught class, it should not be the sole reason. In addition, an academic or pre-academic skill should always be addressed.

Co-Teachers' Levels of Participation May Vary

The final element in defining co-teaching concerns participation. This topic affects professionals in secondary schools more than those in elementary schools. Many special educators have a background in elementary education or licensure in a single secondary subject area, and yet they may be asked to co-teach in several subjects or in a subject which they have not had focused study. In these cases, it is particularly important to discuss what each person's contribution will be. The special educator may not deliver half the instruction, but some clear roles should be outlined. Could the special educator open the class with a brief review of material covered the day before? Take a lead in giving directions? Insert a learning strategy into the instruction to be covered through a brief lecture? Co-teachers address this topic in hundreds of creative ways when it is pertinent. In fact, there is only one clearly unacceptable approach...and that is to have the special educator take a completely passive role during instruction until he or she "feels comfortable" with the material. Although that option might occur for a specific lesson, if it is the pattern then the class is not co-taught, and the matter of whether it is worth having two teachers there should be raised.

Varying participation may, across all grade levels, also pertain to the chores related to teaching. If one special educator co-teaches in three or four classrooms per day, it is not realistic to expect that person to do half the grading, half the bulletin boards, or half the preparation of materials. No formula can determine how chores should be divided, but this topic is covered in more detail in Chapter 4.

Before leaving the definition of co-teaching, a final word of clarification is in order. You may live in a state or district where different terminology is used. Your state might use language that is in NCLB and have *consultative teaching* or *collaborative teaching* or both. The role of the special educator might be called *classroom support teacher* or another term. Such variations will always exist, and it is not possible to address in one book all the variations that may be created. What is critical is that you understand the core concepts that underlie co-teaching so that you can recognize what it makes possible for students and realize the level of commitment that you need to make it succeed.

What Co-Teaching is Not

So many misconceptions about co-teaching exist and so many professionals are using the term *co-teaching* for such a wide variety of arrangements that it is as important to clarify what co-teaching is *not* as it is to clearly define it. Here are a few examples of what co-teaching is not:

- Co-teaching is not having an extra set of hands in the classroom. In co-teaching, both professionals are considered integral to the instructional process, and both have essential teaching roles.

- Co-teaching is not one person (usually the general education teacher) teaching while the other person (usually the special education teacher) roams around the classroom to provide assistance to students who need help with spelling words or comprehending directions, or to address student behavior issues. Although providing assistance may be one component of a co-taught class, a topic addressed in Chapter 3, when one professional continually plays the role of the classroom helper, the entire notion of an instructional partnership is undermined.

- Co-teaching is not an arrangement where one person takes the lead teaching on Monday and the other on Tuesday. Variations of this misunderstanding are exchanging lead roles by week or by instructional unit. This type of turn-taking, usually a response to limited planning time, creates a classroom that has little more intensity than a class with one teacher because the richness of shared teaching often is lost. In this instance the fact that each teacher leads does not eliminate the fact that one of the teachers typically is functioning as an assistant.

- Co-teaching is not a convenient means for busy educators to get out-of-class responsibilities completed. For example, although all professionals have emergencies that call them from the classroom and days when the duplicating just did not get completed, co-teaching should not be used as a mechanism for one professional to work on grading or make phone calls while the other teaches. The point of co-teaching is taking advantage of both professionals' knowledge and skills, and that requires that both teachers be present and fully engaged in the teaching/learning process.

Co-Teaching and Related Terms

All too often in education, the terms used to describe practices are not clearly defined. Perhaps partly because co-teaching is still evolving, it sometimes is given other labels that actually are about related—but distinct—concepts and practices. In this section, co-teaching is distinguished from three of the most commonly confused terms: collaboration, inclusion, and team teaching.

Collaboration

Did you think that the *co* in co-teaching stood for collaborative? Actually, it simply refers to the joint nature of this service delivery model. And although effective co-teaching includes collaboration, the two terms are not synonyms. Collaboration is a very broad term that refers to *how* professionals work together—in schools, or in any other endeavor, such as social services, business, and medicine. As Friend and Cook (2007) note, collaboration is a *style* for interaction that is based on

- mutual goals
- parity
- voluntariness
- shared responsibility for key decisions
- shared accountability for outcomes, and
- shared resources.

Further, collaboration is developmental, beginning with the belief by each participant that what is done together can be better than what anyone could do alone and including the growth of trust and respect and a sense of community.

One straightforward way to illustrate collaboration is to think about a school situation such as this one: Two professionals have been told they are to co-teach during the upcoming school year. When they have a chance to meet, the general education teacher says, "I didn't agree to this; I was assigned. And I understand that you do not have much background in social studies. Since I'm the one responsible for the test scores in the class, I think it would be best if you did things that would help the kids but not interfere with the flow of instruction—take notes, make sure the kids are paying attention. Then when I finish, you can help your students if they need it. OK?" As you might guess, this diatribe is anything but collaborative. It uses a very directive style. The classroom teacher has made it clear that she does not see a shared goal, that her participation is not voluntary, that she will be in charge (thus undermining parity), and that decision-making and outcomes are not shared.

But what if the teacher had said this? "I didn't sign up for co-teaching and I'm not sure I even understand what we are supposed to be doing. But I suspect the administrators are counting on us to figure out how to make this work, so I'm willing to give it a try. How do you see two teachers working together in one classroom? One thing that I see we need to consider is how to fit your expertise on reaching students with disabilities with my expertise in social studies. I'm anxious to hear your ideas and see what we can accomplish." The content and tone of this message is completely different. Even though the teacher was assigned to the teaching arrangement, working together is a choice she has made and exemplified voluntariness. Further, the teacher is communicating the presence of shared goals, decision-making, and accountability. Respect has been communicated as have the beginnings of trust and sense of community.

The strongest co-teaching is highly collaborative, but collaboration applies to many situations in addition to co-teaching (Fishbaugh, 1997; Friend & Cook, 1990). Middle school teams should be collaborative, as should grade level teams in elementary schools and departments in high schools. Similarly, intervention assistance teams rely on collaboration as do school leadership teams. If you remember that collaboration is a means for accomplishing the work at hand, you'll understand that co-teaching is just one type of work enhanced by the interpersonal style of collaboration.

Inclusion

In your school, are co-teaching and inclusion sometimes used as synonyms? Are classrooms where co-teaching is implemented called inclusion classrooms? Do staff members sometimes refer to "doing inclusion" (as in, "We do inclusion in fourth grade but not in fifth," or "We do inclusion in the basic English class but not honors English") when what they mean is that they are implementing (or not implementing) co-teaching?

Separating the concepts of co-teaching and inclusion is critical because they are very different from each other. As you learned earlier in this chapter, co-teaching is a service delivery option, a way to provide to students with disabilities or other special needs the special instruction to which they are entitled while ensuring that they can access the general curriculum in the least restrictive environment.

Inclusion is not a service delivery option. Inclusion is a belief system or philosophy that guides all the practices in any specific school. In fact, the smallest meaningful unit for inclusiveness is the school. There is no such thing as an inclusion class, an inclusion teacher, or—sadly—inclusion students. All these terms imply that inclusion is about where students sit during the school day. General education placement certainly is part of inclusive schooling, but it is just one dimension of it. In an inclusive school, all staff members believe that it is their job to provide the best education for all students, respecting their pupils' diversity and maximizing their potential. They believe that full participation with peers is the strong preference and make decisions that move away from general education placement only after thoughtful deliberation, but the goal is always membership in the same learning community. Highly inclusive schools have some pullout services available to students for whom it is necessary, but that pullout is guided by data-based decisions, revisited often, and continued only for as long as necessary. Conversely, in schools where professionals proclaim, "We're an inclusion school—we never pull any students out," it is unlikely that inclusive practices exist. In these schools, only a single means of addressing students' needs is being used, and that is unlikely to be adequate.

How do inclusion and co-teaching fit together? Co-teaching as a service delivery option is one way that students in inclusive schools may receive their services. But it is not the only way. As noted earlier in this chapter, some students may be served through consultation, that is, indirect services. Other students may receive some service in separate settings, either in combination with co-teaching or in place of it. The bias is always in favor of general education placement, but even more importantly, the needs of individual students are the first consideration.

Team Teaching

You may find that *co-teaching* and *team teaching* are sometimes used interchangeably, but two factors distinguish these terms and are reasons to understand their differences.

The first distinguishing feature of co-teaching versus team teaching concerns the number of students in the class group. Examples of team teaching throughout its rather lengthy history (for example, Warwick, 1971) typically have been characterized as keeping a constant student teacher ratio. That is, when team teaching was introduced in the 1950s as a high school model called the Trump Plan (Friend, Reising, & Cook, 1993; Geen, 1985), it involved high school general education teachers combining multiple sections of a course so that one master teacher would deliver instruction and then the other teachers would facilitate discussion and other class activities. When three teachers were involved, the arrangement would include approximately 75 students. Team teaching later was applied to elementary open-concept schools in which teams of approximately four teachers would share responsibility for teaching 100 students. Again, the student-teacher ratio was a constant. Even today, team teaching often is used in reference to middle schools where the 25-to-1 student:teacher ratio still is in place. It also sometimes describes high school courses that are interdisciplinary such as an American studies class that teaches history through literature by blending a section of the history class with a section of a literature class so that the teachers can collaborate on instruction.

Co-teaching is very different. In co-teaching, the teacher:student ratio is dramatically reduced. That is, a class of 25 students with one teacher might be changed to a class of 25 students, five of whom have disabilities, and two teachers for part or all of the school day. Changing the teacher:student ratio from 1:25 to 1:12.5 makes the classroom a very different teaching/learning environment, one that cannot be accomplished in team teaching.

The second difference between co-teaching and team teaching concerns teacher expertise. In most of the professional literature that has addressed team teaching over the past five decades, team teaching has been carried out by two general education teachers. Co-teaching presumes that the two professionals have very different types of skills. This raises the question of each teacher's contribution. Here is one way to think about this.

General education teachers have these four areas of primary expertise:

1. **Curriculum and instruction**. General education teachers must hold knowledge of what needs to be taught, in what order, and how this content fits into the larger curriculum picture.

2. **Classroom management**. General education teachers always get their students in relatively large groups. They must be highly skilled at getting all the students engaged, keeping them engaged, and doing this while addressing their various learning needs.

3. **Knowledge of typical students.** These teachers have a good sense of whether student learning or social/behavioral functioning is within the parameters they expect. Although some teachers make mistakes in this arena, classroom teachers generally make sound judgments about whether students are simply struggling or may have a disability. Remember that general education teachers make most of the referrals for students eventually identified as having disabilities.

4. **Pacing**. General education teachers have to know how to get through the curriculum in the time allocated. Particularly in this age of accountability, this is an essential skill. They are vigilant to be sure that all essential skills for the grade level or subject are introduced to students so that they are prepared for high stakes testing and other assessments.

Of course, these are not the only skills that general educators possess, nor is it true that special educators do not have any of these skills. The point is that general educators, as a whole, have a specific set of priorities that are central to their role.

However, the same can be said for special educators and other specialists. Here are the four primary areas of expertise for special educators:

1. **Process of learning**. Whether a special educator works with young children or students about to leave high school and regardless of the specific disabilities those students have, the goal of the special educator is to help their students learn how to learn. That is, they provide learners with strategies, accommodations, and modifications to facilitate learning, and they offer remediation or developmental specialized instruction.

2. **Individualization**. As professionals, special educators are trained to focus separately on each student and to design and deliver exactly what that student needs. The Individuals with Disabilities Education Improvement Act of 2004 (IDEA) has as its foundation this notion of individualizing, as noted in the requirement that each student receiving special education must have an IEP.

3. **Paperwork**. Although all teachers complete paperwork, the paperwork for special educators tends to be more extensive than that for general education teachers. In addition, the paperwork—IEPs, other student records, test reports, documentation of parent contacts, and so on—can have legal ramifications, and so it must receive focused attention from the special educators.

4. **Emphasis on mastery versus coverage, with pacing as a secondary consideration**. Even in this era of increased accountability, special educators tend to prioritize helping students to truly master specific concepts and skills, even if it means not getting to all the content that is supposed to be addressed. Their rationale is that students whose understanding is incomplete are unlikely to be able to use the information and also unlikely to succeed in the next level of learning.

As was true in the discussion about general educators' skills, these are priorities. They are not the only skills that special educators possess, nor is it true that general educators have none of these skills.

Now the second difference between co-teaching and team teaching can be highlighted. In team teaching, when two general educators with similar expertise and priorities work together, they usually share expectations. They worry about getting through the curriculum, raising achievement, and preparing students for high stakes testing, all appropriate and understandable goals. If two special educators taught together, they probably would spend considerable time addressing each student's special needs, documenting learning and stressing mastery.

But consider what should happen when a special educator or specialist partners with a general education teacher. The differences in their professional orientation and emphasis should lead to key differences in how each would approach instruction—and the result should be heated discussion, lively arguments, and a classroom in which instruction reflects the blended best of each perspective. That is, one teacher may want to speed up the pacing while the other expresses concern about the level of understanding of several students and volunteers to find some supplemental materials for them. One teacher may stress completing assignments independently while the other sees a need for coaching some students and providing scaffolding for student learning. One teacher may set an expectation for all members of the class while the other teacher notes that one student is living in particularly difficult circumstances and needs special consideration.

The differences between the educators who co-teach are perhaps its most powerful dimension. Co-teaching at its best is about forging new types of instruction because of the strengths that each educator brings to the classroom.

Co-Teaching and Paraprofessionals

Professionals often ask how paraprofessionals fit into programs that emphasize co-teaching. The question is a valid one that should be addressed, but it also can be a slightly complicated one.

The simple answer is that paraprofessionals are valuable school personnel who provide support in the classroom, but they do not co-teach. Distinguishing what paraprofessionals do from what teachers do is critical.

Paraprofessionals who support students in general education settings can be asked to work with small groups of students, lead for selected students a review of concepts already taught, and assist a teacher in monitoring student attention, behavior, and work. However, they should not be asked to lead large-group instruction, plan and deliver initial instruction, interpret assessment results, make instructional decisions, or assume primary or sole responsibility for a group of students over an extended period of time (French, 2003). In other words, they can support a classroom and may even carry out some activities that occur in co-teaching, but it is inappropriate to expect a paraprofessional to be a co-teacher.

Similar comments could be made for classroom volunteers. When an individual is not employed as a licensed professional, co-teaching is not an option. Conversely, other licensed professionals, including speech/language therapists, psychologists, and counselors, can and sometimes do co-teach.

To keep all of this clear, some school staff members are beginning to use different terms for these two arrangements. *Co-teaching* is used to refer to arrangements in which licensed professionals are actually sharing in instructional delivery. *Supporting* is used to refer to situations in which a non-licensed individual (or individual employed in a non-licensed capacity) assists in a classroom, or a licensed professional is present only to assist specific students with a limited overall classroom role.

Distinguishing the roles and responsibilities of paraprofessionals and special educators is not in any way intended to minimize the valuable assistance that paraprofessionals offer in the general education setting. Rather, it is to protect them from being asked to carry out, in essence, the job of a teacher—with nearly all parts of that job except the salary. At the same time, the distinctions are intended to clarify that professionals should be actively involved in all aspects of the instructional process, that they should *not* be functioning like paraprofessionals. Figure 1.1 provides some examples of appropriate tasks and activities for paraprofessionals working in general education classrooms on behalf of students with disabilities.

Entire books have been written about paraprofessionals. You should access such resources for detailed information if you work with these essential personnel. Keep in mind, though, that even if the paraprofessionals in your district or school are trained to carry out a remedial reading or math program, their work is not to take the place of that of teachers.

Components for Successful Co-Teaching

Now that you have learned what co-teaching is and is not, how it relates to other terms often used in today's schools, and how paraprofessionals' work relates to co-teaching, one additional set of concepts can help refine your understanding and provide direction for your co-teaching program. During the early 1990s, an extensive research project was undertaken in Colorado to capture essential elements of co-teaching (for example, Adams & Cessna, 1991). Interviewing many pairs of experienced co-teachers and following up on that initial research with a detailed study of successful and unsuccessful co-teaching partnerships, the researchers found that five key components must be in place for co-teaching, components that have been validated repeatedly. Each component is briefly described below, and an activity related to each is included in the appendix at the end of this chapter.

Shared Philosophy

Effective co-teachers have a shared philosophy of teaching and learning, one that reflects their priorities and beliefs. This shared philosophy needs to extend beyond general statements such as "All children can learn" and "The job of teachers is to take students from where they are as far as they can go." Instead, the shared philosophy is more about the core beliefs that each teacher has about the ways that teaching and learning should occur, student behavior, and professionals' responsibilities. For example, one teacher may believe that assignments changed for any student should carry a minor grade penalty. The other teacher may argue

Figure 1.1
Paraprofessionals Who Support Students with Disabilities in General Education: Examples of Tasks and Activities

- Re-read with students in a one-to-one arrangement stories or other materials after they have been introduced by a teacher.
- Review concepts already taught to students who have not completely grasped them.
- Provide drill-and-practice type activities for vocabulary, math facts, and similar instructional items.
- Maintain files related to students with disabilities, including portfolios being used for assessment purposes.
- Read aloud test items for students entitled to this assessment accommodation, following directions given by a techer.
- Grade tests or other student work using a key or detailed rubric.
- Work with students with disabilities in small groups that include peers without disabilities for the purpose of fostering social interactions.
- Prepare instructional materials needed for the class based on a sample or detailed directions provided by a teacher.
- Provide personal assistance to students as needed, including moving students from place to place, positioning them, helping them with personal care, and supporting them in other daily activities such as eating and dressing.
- As directed by a teacher, collect and record data related to specific students or groups of students (for example, concerning behavior for a student on a behavior intervention plan).
- As permitted by policies and directed by a teacher, provide supervision to students changing classes or moving from one location in the school to another.
- Facilitate the use of assistive technology, which may include assisting the student to use equipment or software and reporting problems related to such items.
- Communicate to the special education teacher matters directly related to students with disabilities that may need teacher-teacher discussion
- Assist teachers in completing many classroom chores such as recording grades, setting up labs, changing bulletin board displays, collecting permission forms, taking attendance, and managing supplies and materials.

that when changes are made to accommodate special needs, no differences should be made in grading. What are other examples of differences in beliefs that could affect co-teaching?

Co-teachers are likely to agree about most of their beliefs, but any differences should be noted, discussed, and possibly negotiated in terms of expectations for students. The key for co-teachers is to make sure that their overall goals are consistent and that their communication is clear. Their differences should be considered a strength, but shared core beliefs are foundational for co-teaching.

Prerequisites

Even before co-teaching begins, prerequisites that each educator brings to the classroom affect co-teaching. Experienced co-teachers report that these are the most important prerequisites:

1. **Personal prerequisites**. Co-teachers should have personal qualities that are supportive of working with colleagues. For example, they need a sense of humor and a willingness to set aside differences once they have been addressed. The most important prerequisite, though, is likely to be the ability to give up control. Teachers by nature tend to be rather controlling. For working with students, this is a positive attribute. However, other adults do not like to be controlled, and co-teachers need to be sure that this potential source of conflict is directly addressed. Even teachers who think they are not controlling should ask their co-teachers about this issue and take any feedback to heart.

2. **Pedagogical prerequisites**. Co-teachers need to generally understand school, teaching, and students. Although not common, when a teacher does not understand the educational process and culture, problems can occur. One example concerns a young special educator who could not seem to function as a teacher instead of a friend to students. That is, he would joke around with students until they became boisterous and then suddenly get angry at them for misbehaving. Despite feedback, coaching, and professional development he could not seem to understand his role as a teacher differed from the role of buddy. He clearly was not ready to co-teach.

3. **Professional prerequisites**. Finally, co-teachers must possess

the specialized expertise that forms the reason for the partnership. General educators should be expert in the four areas mentioned earlier in this chapter, and special educators should be expert in their four areas. Although all educators learn from each other through co-teaching and usually become better educators because of it, co-teaching is premised on participants having a firm grounding in their own areas of knowledge and skill.

Collaborative Relationship

Earlier in this chapter, collaboration was distinguished from co-teaching. However, experienced co-teachers stress that co-teaching truly is a collaborative relationship and, as such, it depends on parity, sharing goals for students, sharing responsibility for key decisions and accountability for outcomes, and resources—the very characteristics of collaboration already introduced. They also note that co-teaching requires the development of trust and respect and a sense of classroom community. Even for co-teachers who intuitively understand the potential of this service delivery option and who enthusiastically implement it, collaboration is developmental. That is, it grows stronger and matures over time.

Clear Plans and Procedures

Co-teachers are most effective when they have specific plans for accomplishing their goals. This topic is addressed in more detail in Chapter 3, *Co-Teaching Approaches,* and Chapter 6, *Logistics,* but a few comments here can provide an overview of this component. Think about what you are doing when you co-teach. You are making a commitment to maintaining the rigorous standards of the curriculum in place in the general education classroom. At the same time, you are challenging advanced learners, maintaining the pace for typical learners, supporting struggling learners, and providing significant accommodations and modifications for students with intense needs. To do all of this requires planfulness both in designing instruction and in carrying it out. Without this planfulness, there is too great a risk that the co-taught classroom will look just like the classroom did before, the only exception being that two adults are present instead of one.

Ultimately, having clear plans and procedures enables the teachers to prepare for instruction that addresses diverse student needs, to deliver that instruction in a way that is respectful to the skills of both teachers and cognizant of the uniqueness of students, and to manage the classroom with efficiency. The importance of this domain is the reason why two full chapters of this book are devoted to various aspects of it.

Supportive Context

Experienced co-teachers indicate that two factors are most essential in creating a context supportive of co-teaching. The first is administrative support. In fact, one co-teacher made this insightful comment: "If your principal only knows one paragraph about co-teaching, it's going to go nowhere." If you are reading this manual as a teacher, you undoubtedly realize the importance of administrative support. If you have it, you know that you can count on your principal to help with scheduling and planning time, problems that occur in the classroom, and parent questions and concerns.

If your principal is not strongly committed to co-teaching as a service option, you may feel like you work in a climate of benign neglect—that is, your principal leaves most decisions to you and really does not take an active role in creating or sustaining the program. In some unfortunate cases, you may feel like you are being asked to do an impossible job. Perhaps your principal was mandated to implement a co-teaching program and is not in favor of it. In those cases, you can only do the best you can, influencing your administrator's opinion when you can but not taking responsibility for the entire program. Many strategies for principals and other administrators to support co-teaching are included in Chapter 7.

The second context factor is professional development. Experienced co-teachers note that although some professionals have wonderful intuitive skills and successfully co-teach without professional development, for co-teaching to be implemented as a standard program option for students with disabilities, educators need to acquire awareness of it, knowledge about it, and skills to implement it. Just as professionals in other disciplines receive training prior to being asked to use a new strategy, it is reasonable for educators to expect to learn about co-teaching instead of just being told to implement it.

With an understanding of all these key concepts that relate to co-teaching, you have the tools to develop an exemplary program or refine the program in which you work. Collaboration is the foundation for such programs since the ability to work together is integral to creating them. In addition, fostering inclusive practices through collaboration creates a context in which co-teaching can thrive. Ultimately, supporting students with disabilities or other special needs through co-teaching can help educators to reach the goals of contemporary schools.

For Further Thought

1. Which of the components of the definition of co-teaching seem most critical to you? What steps could you, your co-teaching partner, and your principal take to ensure that co-teaching at your school incorporates each of these components?

2. How do the explanations of co-teaching, collaboration, inclusion, and team teaching presented in this chapter compare to your previous understandings? How is each of these terms used in your school or district's policy documents or procedure manuals, IEP forms, and informal conversations? Why is it important to distinguish among them? What steps could be taken to align the concepts or terms with practices?

3. What is the role of paraprofessionals in providing support to students with disabilities in your school? What changes would you suggest to maximize their impact on student learning? What are the questions and professional development needs that general education teachers have concerning the work of paraprofessionals?

4. Experienced co-teachers report that a shared philosophy, individual prerequisites, collaboration, specific classroom practices, and a supportive context are essential for co-teaching success. To what extent is each of these components in place for you and your co-teacher? How could you use the different points of view that you each bring to co-teaching to make your partnership stronger and improve outcomes for your students?

Taking Action

1. At a faculty, team, or department meeting, ask teachers to jot down their understandings of each of the terms presented in this chapter. Use their responses as the basis for a conversation about current practices in the school and actions that could be taken to improve those practices.

2. Make a commitment to eliminate the divisive language of "my kids" and "your kids." For example, professionals could decide to assess a 25-cent fine against anyone who speaks in this way; the money could be given to charity at the end of the school year. Another idea is to encourage all staff members to say, "no, OUR kids" whenever the my/your language is used. Remember, when the language divides students the practices are likely to do the same.

3. In secondary schools, start now to get both teachers' names listed on class schedules and grade reports. It's not a two-teacher classroom unless both teachers' names are included. This is critical for establishing parity. If the concern is related to accountability and highly qualified teacher status, simply list the person who is highly qualified in the content area first (and note that practice in a policy manual). If the concern relates to putting two names in the electronic field, talk to a programmer for creative solutions. While solutions are explored, be sure that both teachers' names are prominently posted somewhere in the classroom.

References

Adams, L., & Cessna, K. (1991). Designing systems to facilitate collaboration: Collective wisdom from Colorado. *Preventing School Failure, 35*(4), 37-42.

Dieker, L. A., & Murawski, W. W. (2003). Co-teaching at the secondary level: Unique issues, current trends, and suggestions for success. *High School Journal, 86*(4), 1-13.

Fishbaugh, M. S. E. (1997). *Models of collaboration.* Boston: Allyn & Bacon.

French, N. K. (2003). Managing paraeducators in our school. Thousand Oaks, CA: Corwin.

Friend, M. (2007). The co-teaching partnership. *Educational Leadership, 64*(5), 48-52.

Friend, M., & Cook, L. (2007). *Interactions: Collaboration skills for school professionals* (5th edition). Boston: Allyn and Bacon.

Friend, M., & Cook, L. (1990). Collaboration as a predictor for success in school reform. *Journal of Educational and Psychological Consultation, 1*(1), 69-86.

Friend, M. & Hurley-Chamberlain, D. (2007, January). Is co-teaching effective? *CEC Today.* Retrieved January 10, 2007 from http://www.cec.sped.org/AM/Template.cfm?Section=Home&TEMPLATE=/CM/ContentDisplay.cfm&CONTENTID=7504.

Friend, M., Reising, M., & Cook, L. (1993). Co-teaching: An overview of the past, a glimpse at the present, and considerations for the future. *Preventing School Failure, 37*(4), 6–10.

Geen, A. G. (1985). Team teaching in the secondary schools of England and Wales. *Educational Review, 37,* 29–38.

Magiera, K., Smith, C., Zigmond, N., & Gebaner, K. (2005). Benefits of co-teaching in secondary mathematics classes. *Teaching Exceptional Children, 37*(3), 20-24.

Mastropieri, M. A., Scruggs, T. E., Graetz, J., Norland, J., Gardizi, W., & McDuffie, K. (2005). Case studies in co-teaching in the content areas: Successes, failures, and challenges. *Intervention in School and Clinic, 40,* 260-270.

Pardini, P. (2006). In one voice: Mainstream and ELL teachers work side-by-side in the classroom, teaching language through content. *Journal of Staff Development, 27*(4), 20-25.

Warwick, D. (1971). *Team teaching.* London: University of London.

Chapter 1 Appendix:
Worksheets for Exploring Co-Teaching
Components

• • • • • •

The worksheets on the following pages are designed to help you explore the five key components of co-teaching. You may decide that you should complete all of them, or you may find just one or two of them helpful for reflecting on co-teaching at your school.

Exploring Classroom Philosophy

Co-teachers should discuss their classroom philosophy, that is, the absolutes that they believe must be in place for education to be effective. Use this worksheet to think about and record your absolutes and then trade ideas with your co-teacher. Consider how you can use areas in which you strongly agree as a basis for building your partnership. Identify topics or beliefs that you may need to discuss further in order to reach agreement on how your beliefs can be respected in the classroom.

When you think about students in the classroom, what are your three absolutes?

1.
2.
3.

What absolutes did your co-teacher list?

1.
2.
3.

When you think about teachers' responsibilities, what are your three absolutes?

1.
2.
3.

What absolutes did your co-teacher list?

1.
2.
3.

When you think about overall classroom climate, what are your three absolutes?

1.
2.
3.

What absolutes did your co-teacher list?

1.
2.
3.

In what areas do we strongly agree? How could we use these shared beliefs to build our partnership?

Individual Prerequisites

Co-teaching is a significantly different way for teachers to approach the task of instructing students. Some educators are excited at the prospect of co-teaching. Others are concerned about the risks and issues that may occur in co-teaching situations. The following activity may assist you to determine your own readiness for co-teaching and provide an understanding of your co-teaching partner's perspective.

My characteristics...	...that are strengths for co-teaching	...that could interfere with co-teaching
Personal traits		
General understandings about schools and students		
Knowledge/skills related to my primary area of expertise		

After you complete the chart above, compare your responses with those of your co-teacher. How can the two of you mix and match your strengths and accommodate your limitations to maximize co-teaching effectiveness?

Collaboration for Co-Teaching

The most successful co-teaching partnerships are highly collaborative. How do you rate yourself on each of these indicators of collaboration? After you complete the worksheet, discuss your responses with your co-teacher.

	Strongly Agree	Neutral		Strongly Disagree	

1. _____ _____ _____ _____ _____ We make time to talk about our co-teaching practice.

2. _____ _____ _____ _____ _____ We take deliberate steps to convey to our students that we have parity.

3. _____ _____ _____ _____ _____ We take deliberate steps to convey parity to our students' parents/families.

4. _____ _____ _____ _____ _____ We can discuss tough issues —- that is, topics on which we disagree.

5. _____ _____ _____ _____ _____ We can raise topics of potential disagreement as soon as they are noted; we do not fret about whether it is safe to do so.

6. _____ _____ _____ _____ _____ We share the same goals for our students.

7. _____ _____ _____ _____ _____ We want to experiment to make co-teaching succeed, even if we did not volunteer for this assignment.

8. _____ _____ _____ _____ _____ We both are responsible for key decisions regarding instruction, classroom management, and student needs.

9. _____ _____ _____ _____ _____ We both are accountable for student outcomes.

10. _____ _____ _____ _____ _____ We each contribute resources to facilitate co-teaching.

11. _____ _____ _____ _____ _____ We try to use our differences to create new options for students.

12. _____ _____ _____ _____ _____ We seek novel solutions to dilemmas rather than just ideas that are owned by either of us.

13. _____ _____ _____ _____ _____ We actively seek ways to draw out each other's strengths while covering for each other's weaknesses.

14. _____ _____ _____ _____ _____ We believe that what we do together in co-teaching is better than what either of us would accomplish separately.

15. _____ _____ _____ _____ _____ Our commitment to co-teaching and trust of each other is growing.

What does your discussion with your co-teacher suggest are areas of strength? Areas for growth?

Classroom Practice

The essence of co-teachign concerns the partnership in the classroom. Although the planning that occurs before co-teaching is crucial as is the evaluation that follows it, a starting point for co-teaching is recognizing the many ways in which teachers' actions and interactions in the classroom can affect their working relationship and their effectiveness in teaching their students. How does each of the topics in the following questions potentially affect co-teaching success?

- How would it be apparent to someone visiting your co-taught class that the instruction is planful? That is, what activities and materials suggest that there is an overall design for instruction but also careful attention to students' individual learning needs?

- What roles and responsibilities does each professional take during instruction in the co-taught classroom?

- What types of messages do teachers tend to send to each other and students when they have few or limited interactions with each other during instruction? When they purposefully engage in instructional conversation? What impact might their interactions have on student learning outcomes?

- How do you and your co-teacher interact with each student? To what extent do all students "belong" fully to both teachers while co-teaching is occurring?

- How do co-teachers make sure that they are both satisfied with the lessons they're teaching and student progress? What strategies do they have to discuss these topics, especially if disagreement is likely?

What strategies are used to address miscommunication or disagreements during instruction? How satisfied are you and your co-teacher with these strategies?

External Supports: The Commitment to Co-Teaching

Co-teaching as a small experimental approach to meeting the needs of just a few students can and often does occur based on the interest of the people involved.

However, if co-teaching is to be an integral part of services to students, the context in which it occurs and the support it receives are critical. To what extent are these external supports available at your school for co-teaching? Note that many of these topics are addressed in detail in other chapters of this manual.

Not at All	Some	To a Great Extent	
_____	_____	_____	1. My principal is knowledgeable about co-teaching.
_____	_____	_____	2. In general, in my school collaborative activities are fostered and valued.
_____	_____	_____	3. My principal takes a leadership role in implementing inclusive practices in my school.
_____	_____	_____	4. Time is made available for planning collaborative activities.
_____	_____	_____	5. School communication between administrators and staff members is clear.
_____	_____	_____	6. Problems and conflicts are identified and directly addressed.
_____	_____	_____	7. "Naysayers" do not have voice over innovators and experimenters.
_____	_____	_____	8. Staff share ideas and information about contemporary issues and best practices for teaching students with disabilities.
_____	_____	_____	9. My school stresses the use of positive approaches for responding to student behavior problems.
_____	_____	_____	10. Shared decision-making is employed at my school.

As you review your answers to this checklist and discuss them with your colleagues, what priorities do they suggest you should set? How can all school staff members, including administrators, work to address matters such as these?

Chapter 2
The Rationale for Co-Teaching

● ● ● ● ● ●

By seeking and blundering we learn.

--Johann Wolfgang Von Goethe

Chapter Objectives

1. Outline legislative factors that are fostering current interest in co-teaching.

2. Analyze research that has examined the process and outcomes of co-teaching and use these studies to discuss the promise and problems of co-teaching as a viable service delivery option for students with disabilities.

3. Address philosophical and anecdotal elements of a rationale for co-teaching.

If your primary interest is in creating or refining your own co-teaching or in assisting your school or district to develop the best co-teaching program possible, you may not be particularly interested in reading about the rationale for co-teaching. You already know it is your goal, you do not sense any need to understand why co-teaching is currently receiving so much attention, and you just want to get on with the many tasks you see ahead.

I hope, though, that you will take time to read the information contained in this chapter. There are several reasons for doing so. First, the information in this chapter can provide you with a bit of historical perspective on co-teaching as it has evolved in special education. In addition, the discussion of legislation related to co-teaching can give you information that might be useful to share with colleagues, parents/families, and community members. Third, reviewing the research on co-teaching can assist you in understanding the empirical basis for this service delivery option and the types of questions that remain to be explored. Finally, the rationale for co-teaching has a philosophical and anecdotal dimension, and that perspective is given voice here.

If you are using this manual for a book study or in conjunction with a graduate class or project, you will find this background information helps to establish context for your emerging knowledge of the status of co-teaching. For individuals in this group, a bibliography of classic and contemporary resources on co-teaching, a few cited in this and other chapters, but many not, is included as the appendix for this chapter. I hope it helps you in your own pursuit of knowledge on this truly exciting option for educating students with disabilities.

The Legislative Basis for Co-Teaching

From 1975 until 2001, educational practices for students with disabilities were guided completely by federal special education law, currently the *Individuals with Disabilities Education Improvement Act* (IDEA) of 2004. Whenever questions arose about the rights of these students and their families, the procedures through which decisions about their education were made, the strategies through which they would be assessed, or the services to which they were entitled, educators looked to IDEA and the many interpretations of it as clarified through litigation.

However, the passage of the *No Child Left Behind Act* (NCLB) drastically changed this approach, especially for schools serving a high number of students who live in poverty. As you undoubtedly know, NCLB now controls many of the most critical elements of educational practices for all students, including those with disabilities and other special needs. It requires that students be taught with methods that have a basis in research, includes nearly all students in mandated assessments, holds school districts accountable for the quality of the education students receive, and provides parents with options for ensuring that their children are able to reach the increasingly high standards being set for learning. The law is controversial, and most professionals object to several of its provisions when applied to students with disabilities. It is beyond the scope of this discussion to address such points of disagreement.

One area in which NCLB has had a significant impact is co-teaching. Further, when NCLB requirements intersect with the traditional principles on which IDEA is based, one strong component of a rationale for co-teaching can be established.

Access to the Curriculum

A fundamental aspect of both IDEA and NCLB is that all students have access to the same rigorous curriculum as other students so that they can reach the high achievement expectations currently being set (Karger & Hitchcock, 2003). Generally, this means that students with disabilities must have involvement in the curriculum dictated by state and local policies for all students.

IDEA's traditional provision of educating students with disabilities in the least restrictive environment (LRE) is the basis for its attention to curriculum access. This law further clarifies this matter by requiring that students' IEPs align with that curriculum and that, in most instances, general education teachers be part of the team that prepares the IEP.

Curriculum access is elaborated upon in other IDEA provisions as well. For example, students' progress in the curriculum must be recorded and communicated to parents at least as often as progress reporting is completed for other students (usually, each grading period). Federal special education law also mandates that supplementary aids and services be provided to students to facilitate their access to curriculum in the general education environment. In addition, it requires that the IEP team write a justification of any decision that removes a student from general education.

Taken together, it is clear that traditional thinking about the need for students with disabilities to spend significant segments (or all) of the school day in a separate setting are changing. A logical response is to ensure that their services are arranged in a way that facilitates that access, and co-teaching has the potential to do this.

Adequate Yearly Progress (AYP)

As you probably know, the achievement expectations for students with disabilities are addressed in NCLB. The law notes that, with the exception of the one percent of students with significant disabilities who complete alternate assessments, students with disabilities should reach proficiency as measured on the same assessments used for other students, with allowed accommodations provided. Many states also have an option for an additional two percent of students to be assessed on grade level standards, but for the assessment to be conducted at a slightly lower level. This latter option was developed as a response to concerns expressed by educational leaders that the achievement bar had been set too high for some students and that an additional assessment strategy was needed.

The expectation for rising student achievement is measured through adequate yearly progress (AYP), usually a percentage set at the state level (that rises each year) to identify the number of students in the state who will be proficient in each subject area. In addition, each state has negotiated what is referred to as a subgroup number that determines for each school and district whether they must consider particular at-risk groups of learners (that is, those who are economically disadvantaged, who represent major racial and ethnic groups, who have disabilities, who are English language learners) separately in judging whether AYP has been achievement. For example, if a state's subgroup for students with disabilities is 20, this generally means that in a school with 20 students with disabilities enrolled, their scores must be disaggregated, or considered separately from those of the rest of students. As a subgroup they must be achieving AYP or the school overall cannot be considered to be achieving AYP. Keep in mind, though, that even if a school's subgroup is too small to be considered separately, this information still is forwarded to the district, state, and federal level, and so it remains critical.

This rather complex provision of NCLB is directly affecting co-teaching. Many professionals are realizing that achieving AYP is far more likely when students with disabilities are educated in the general education setting because they then, as noted earlier, gain access to the same curriculum as other students. Although many special educators have provided this level of instruction in the special education setting, concern exists that it is difficult to maintain the pace of instruction there and that, as a result, students lose critical access.

It should be noted that some special educators who teach in a separate setting resent this notion and emphasize that their instruction covers the same material with the same rigor as occurs in general education. The point is not to debate this issue with any individual teacher—it is to understand that this provision of the law was designed to ensure that all students (regardless of which particular teachers they have) can make AYP.

Highly Qualified Teachers

A third provision of both NCLB and IDEA concerns the necessity of all students being taught in the content areas by teachers who are highly qualified. Like most other parts of NCLB, this requirement is complex. Essentially, it means that teachers of students at the elementary age level and those whose learning skills are at that level (that is, older students with significant intellectual disabilities) must demonstrate that they have the knowledge and skills of elementary educators. All teachers of students at the middle and high school, including special educators, generally must be highly qualified in any core subject area in which they provide initial instruction to students. Specific requirements for being considered highly qualified vary tremendously across states, and special educators also must be highly qualified to deliver special education services.

For special educators at elementary schools, the issue of being highly qualified usually is not significant. These professionals often have licensure in elementary education, or they are considered to possess that knowledge and those skills. At the middle and high school levels, special educators in some states have been determined to be highly qualified to teach in all subject areas, and so their roles have not changed. In other states, special education teachers are prohibited from offering separate sections of core subject courses (for example, English just for students with disabilities) unless they hold licensure or otherwise are highly qualified in that subject. The result of the legislative provision of being highly qualified is an increase in co-teaching interest. The reason is straightforward: If students with disabilities are enrolled in a general education class with co-teaching as their special education service, they are guaranteed to be taught by a teacher highly qualified in the core subject area—the general educator, but they also receive services from a highly qualified (in special education) teacher who meets their unique needs.

Many variations of co-teaching policies can be found related to the matter of highly qualified teachers, and you should consider this brief overview just that, a sketch of the general requirements and not a detailed explanation. If you have questions about being highly qualified, you definitely should ask an authoritative source in your state, possibly a university or state licensure official or a human resources staff member in your school district.

Current legislation has had a profound impact on the education of students with disabilities. In your district you may find that these changes have had a positive impact for students, but you also may find that they are creating challenges difficult to overcome. Whatever your view, co-teaching has become more common as a result.

Research on Co-Teaching

Much of what has been written about co-teaching consists of descriptions of successful and not-so-successful programs, suggestions for addressing the practical issues of establishing co-teaching programs, or advice on how to improve co-teaching arrangements. Over the past several years, though, a body of research has been emerging that directly addresses various aspects of co-teaching. Although still limited in scope and depth, this scholarly work generally considers three aspects of co-teaching:

- Studies of the impact of co-teaching on student outcomes and studies addressing students' and parents' perceptions of it
- Studies of the relationships and practices of teachers in co-taught classrooms
- Studies of program structure and administration

Because the overall purpose of this book is to assist educators in establishing and sustaining co-teaching programs, it is not possible to complete an exhaustive review of co-teaching research in this chapter. What follows are examples of the types of research being conducted and a brief discussion of how they are contributing to the evolution of co-teaching practices.

Co-Teaching and Students

If the primary goal of co-teaching is to ensure that students with disabilities have access to the curriculum and can succeed in it, you might think that most research about it would emphasize this topic. For many reasons that is not the case. For example, to study whether co-teaching is more effective for students with disabilities than a general education class with no co-teaching or a special education class covering comparable content, many variables have to be controlled. Are the teachers teaching in approximately the same manner for the same length of time using similar strategies? Are the students in each group similar in terms of their abilities, needs, and backgrounds? Is the content comparable? Are assessments comparable and focused enough to discern what could be relatively small differences in student performance? Addressing all these factors makes it extraordinarily difficult to study co-teaching in a manner that would be considered rigorous in terms of research standards, and so few studies of this type can be found to date. An alternative is to use qualitative approaches that simultaneously consider many factors and identify patterns in the practices—but may not compare classroom groups to one another.

Even studies that consider students' and families' perspectives on co-teaching are relatively rare. This may be the result of the newness of focused attention on co-teaching and the common pattern in special education: Studies that explore student and family perceptions generally lag behind research on the implementation of new programs and services.

Here are examples of studies of co-teaching related to students and parents:

- Rea, McLaughlin, and Walther-Thomas (2002) studied the programs and services for students with learning disabilities in two middle schools, one that emphasized co-teaching and one that used two elective courses. They found that students in the co-taught classes received significantly higher report card grades in language arts, mathematics, science, and social studies. Their scores on their state tests were comparable, but on the required eighth-grade administration of the *Iowa Test of Basic Skills,* students in co-taught classes scored at significantly higher levels in both language arts and math. Records of in-school and out-of-school suspensions suggested no differences between the groups (which the authors noted as indicative of the fact that students could manage the added stress of being taught in a large group setting), but students in the co-taught classes attended school a significantly higher number of days than the students in the traditional program.

- Wilson and Michaels (2006) conducted a survey of students with disabilities and typical classmates who were enrolled in middle school and high school English classes. The survey included numerical ratings of various aspects of co-teaching as well as open-ended questions so that students would write about their perceptions. Both groups of students were favorable toward co-teaching. Students with disabilities recognized that co-teaching gave them access to the curriculum in a way not available in a special education setting, and they indicated that their skills had improved because of co-teaching. Typical classmates reported that co-teaching enabled them to develop higher levels of abstract thinking and enhanced their literacy skill development. Students also commented on aspects of co-teaching they did not like, including the fact that they could not work on homework from other classes because a teacher would notice.

- Spanning elementary, middle, and high school, Gerber and Popp (1999) interviewed 123 students and their parents concerning co-teaching. They found that both students and their parents were positive about co-teaching. Students with disabilities indicated that they were earning better grades in the co-taught classes and that their organizational skills had improved. Parents of these students stated that they had a clear understanding of the co-teaching program and perceived it had a positive impact on their children's achievement and self-esteem.

Co-Teaching and Teachers

Most research related to co-teaching has addressed teacher perceptions of their partnerships, including their roles and the dilemmas they encounter related to those roles, and the ways in which they conduct their shared classes. Early studies on these topics tended to be very general, without any confirmation that the practices the teachers were using would be considered valid as co-teaching. More recent efforts often blend observation of the teachers with questionnaires and/or interviews. These studies capture more than any other type of research the complexity of co-teaching. Interestingly, though, most research of this sort has emphasized middle and high school co-teaching. This is probably because the challenges of establishing classroom partnerships typically are much greater at those grade levels than in elementary schools.

- Mastropieri, Scruggs, Graetz, Norland, Gardizi, and McDuffie (2005) reported the results of four long-term qualitative case studies of co-teaching in science and social studies. Using interviews, observations, videotapes, and other data, they found a wide range of responses to co-teaching. For example, in some cases, co-teaching was seen as extremely effective in helping students with disabilities succeed in general education settings. In others, challenges such as the pressure that occurred related to high stakes testing limited student access to co-teaching and its perceived success. One factor that strongly influenced classroom practices was the level of content knowledge of the special educator. Special educators generally did not have comparable knowledge of the subject matter; the researchers found that this tended to place them in the role of being an assistant while the general educator clearly became the lead teacher. The extent to which the teachers established a strong positive working relationship also was related to perceived co-teaching success.

- Keefe, Moore and Duff (2004) interviewed high school teachers to study their perceptions of co-teaching. They found that the teachers identified three themes that described their practices: the nature of the collaboration, the roles and responsibilities of the teachers, and the outcomes for students. These professionals believed that co-teachers should have a voice in choosing their teaching partners, and they noted that teachers' ability to get along was a critical factor in co-teaching success. The professionals also indicated that direct conversations about roles and responsibilities in the classroom would have helped them avoid some problems, particularly the dilemma of the special educator functioning more as a classroom assistant than a teaching partner. Like teachers in other studies, they mentioned the importance of content knowledge for special educators. Despite the dilemmas encountered, these co-teachers perceived co-teaching as positive for students with disabilities in terms of less stigma and higher achievement. None of these teachers reported negative outcomes from co-teaching, although special educators were concerned that decisions about students' services be made on an individual basis.

- Weiss and Lloyd (2003) also observed middle and high school co-teachers and interviewed them concerning their perceptions and practices. In a sample that included six classrooms, these researchers found that special educator roles in general education classrooms varied tremendously. In some cases they functioned as assistants, while in others they taught content or even removed groups of students from the classroom to teach in a separate setting. Other factors influencing the success of co-teaching included scheduling (the number of classes that special educators were expected to support) and general education teachers' attitudes toward this service delivery arrangement.

Co-Teaching Program Structure and Administration

Some researchers are interested in the ways in which co-teaching programs are structured, staffed, and administered. However, this type of information often is gathered as part of a larger study of teachers and students, or it is part of a study about overall inclusive practices, not just co-teaching. For example, in the study by Weiss and Lloyd (2003) just described, it was found that special educators felt pressured to participate in co-teaching by principals and the community, but that the supports necessary for its success did not accompany this pressure. This area of study is particularly important as school administrators plead for "successful models." However, it is unlikely that research about program structure will ever fully address their needs because the way a program is structured and managed is dependent on many school-specific elements.

Here are two studies that have directly examined programmatic and administrative matters related to co-teaching.

- Salisbury and McGregor (2002) examined the administrative climate and context of five successful inclusive elementary schools in three states. Using a school climate questionnaire, observations by on-site liaisons, and interviews with principals, they found several shared elements key to the schools' success. First, the principals of these schools were risk-takers who reflected on their actions. They were clear in their beliefs and firm in their expectations of teachers for making the belief system a reality. In addition, they recognized the value of professional relationships, and they were accessible and willing to share decision making with staff members. Finally, these administrators were intentional—that is, they knew the goals they were working toward and used those goals to guide their work. They did not let obstacles divert their efforts; instead, they worked to overcome any challenges encountered.

- Burnstein, Sears, Wilcoxen, Cabello, and Spagna (2004) looked at a school change model they implemented over a period of three years in two school districts moving toward inclusive practices. They interviewed administrators, teachers, and parents to gather data. Although their focus was not specifically co-teaching, their results help to inform co-teaching program development. They found that the schools in these districts implemented changes in very different ways: All became more inclusive, but some schools relied heavily on co-teaching, some kept a mix of traditional pullout and co-teaching practices but increased opportunities for students with disabilities to participate in general education classes, and some schools expanded inclusiveness to address the needs of students with significant disabilities. One significant conclusion was that all schools expressed as a priority keeping available an array of service options for meeting student needs.

If you ask any professional who is a student of research on co-teaching, you will hear that efforts to date have been limited and that more data are needed regarding nearly every aspect of it. The studies just mentioned are evidence of the validity of that perception. However, the number of studies appearing has increased dramatically over the past several years, and if that trend continues, the research basis for co-teaching should become clearer.

Philosophical and Anecdotal Evidence for Co-Teaching

Long before NCLB and its influence on IDEA created the current impetus for co-teaching, special educators were proposing that students with disabilities could succeed in general education classrooms if their teachers forged partnerships so that both high expectations and individualized support could be addressed there. As early as the 1980s (for example, Garvar & Papania, 1982; Bauwens, Hourcade, & Friend, 1989), the concept of co-teaching was beginning to appear in the professional literature as an alternative to traditional, usually separate, special education service delivery models, one that conveyed optimism about the potential of blending the best of general education and special education (Epanchin & Friend, 2007).

Early writing about co-teaching reflected the growing trend of inclusive practices, and it represented a critical phase in the process of re-conceptualizing special education from being viewed as a *place* to being recognized as a *service*. Looking back, it should not have been surprising that this type of thinking would emerge. As early as the 1960s, Lloyd Dunn (1968) had questioned whether separate special education services were effective in improving outcomes for students with disabilities. His thinking was clearly incorporated into the least restrictive environment (LRE) provision of the 1975 Education of the Handicapped Act (Public Law 94-142, now IDEA), a provision still in place and already discussed earlier in this chapter. Dunn's thinking was re-iterated and extended in 1986 by Madeline Will, then Assistant Secretary of the U.S. Office of Special Education and Rehabilitation Services, when she called for a regular education initiative (REI) in which general and special educators would collaborate to educate students with disabilities along with their typical peers (Will, 1986).

The components of a rationale for co-teaching that came from this time period are still relevant today, and include (a) increased educational opportunities for all students, (b) less fragmentation in students' education; (c) a reduction in the stigma associated with being identified as having a disability; and (d) a stronger system of support among the adults responsible for educating students.

Increasing Educational Opportunities

The first part of the traditional rationale for co-teaching concerns the opportunities it creates for all students. That is, in co-taught classes a first concern is to provide to students with disabilities options that otherwise would not exist. For students with mild to moderate disabilities this notion relates to learning the traditional curriculum. For students with significant disabilities this idea originally related to enhancing opportunities for interactions with typical classmates for the purpose of enhancing social skills. Today, of course, access to achieving academic goals are a key consideration.

In a co-taught class, students who are gifted and talented should have more options for developing their extraordinary abilities. They should be able to demonstrate their mastery of the planned instruction and pursue their interests or add depth to their learning by extending their understandings. The presumption is that with two teachers, a place can be made in the instruction to move beyond what is intended for the majority of the learners.

At the same time, students who struggle to learn but who are not eligible for special education also should be given the supports they need in order to succeed. Though clear data on this group of students have not been reported, many educators have always believed that these at-risk learners are the ones who may reap the most incidental benefit from co-teaching. That is, the many strategies and techniques that special educators know and use to enhance the learning of students with disabilities are just as effective for these students. In co-teaching, they receive the advantages of those strategies and techniques that would otherwise be unavailable to them.

Some educators also comment that a final group profiting from co-teaching includes average learners. These students may not require extraordinary attention, and so in a one-teacher classroom they may be overlooked. In co-teaching, though, the likelihood increases that they will be members of small learning groups, that they will have more opportunities to interact with the teachers, and that their less dramatic learning needs will be noticed and addressed.

Decreasing Educational Fragmentation

The second component of a traditional rationale for co-teaching concerns educational fragmentation and pertains in various forms to both elementary and secondary educational settings. In elementary schools, students who leave a general education setting to receive special education or related services typically miss small amounts of instructional time that may add up to be significant. That is, if a student spends a total of 12 minutes per day packing up, walking down the hall, waiting for the special educator to be available to begin instruction, settling down, and then reversing this process at the end of the session, an hour per week of instructional time would be lost. The impact of moving students between settings is that those who need the most instructional time receive the least time among all the students in a school. Co-teaching can eliminate this dilemma. Further, students have missed instruction while in the special education setting, and it can happen that no mechanism is in place to help them learn what was missed and connect the instruction presented in the special education setting to that in the general education setting.

For students in middle and high school, fragmentation relates to lost opportunities. That is, if students are assigned to receive special education services as part of their schedule, those services may be in lieu of courses that other students can take. One example is foreign language, and the impact can be significant. If middle school students take Spanish, but students with disabilities receive special education supports during that time, the latter group will be behind when it is time to take Spanish in high school. For a college-bound student with a disability, this may present a challenge that is very difficult to overcome.

The notion of lost instructional time and program fragmentation has changed somewhat with current legislation, especially because of the highly qualified teacher requirement. However, it still makes a crucial point: When separate services are being considered, the costs of those services to the student's learning are as important to weigh as the benefits.

Reducing Stigma

Experienced educators know that some students, especially those in middle or high school, may dread being assigned to a special education class (even parttime) because of the stigma associated with it. They may report that classmates call them names and that teachers presume they cannot learn, all because of their disability labels and their participation in a separate education. One goal of co-teaching is to reduce or eliminate this stigma by making education seamless and the disability part of the learning variations that can be found in any classroom.

Of course, reducing stigma depends largely on the way in which co-teaching is implemented. If the special educator in the general education classroom mostly hovers near the students with disabilities to be sure they are paying attention, completing their work, and behaving appropriately, the stigma is increased instead of decreased. In contrast, if co-teachers use approaches such as those outlined in Chapter 3, stigma associated with disability labeling can largely be avoided.

Creating a Professional Support System

The final element of a traditional rationale for co-teaching concerns the professionals. Like most of the topics discussed in this chapter section, few data exist to document the extent of this result of co-teaching, but it is important to mention nonetheless. For decades, teaching has been characterized as a lonely profession (Lortie, 1975), one in which isolation is the norm and collaboration is still not integral (Barth, 2006). Co-teaching can play a role in changing that. In fact, experienced co-teachers report that the camaraderie of a classroom partnership is energizing and comforting. That is, co-teachers relate that co-teaching helps them renew their commitment to teaching and inspires them to generate new ideas for reaching their students. They also comment that a teaching partner provides another important perspective on students, classroom procedures, instruction, and discipline.

Across the country, countless general education and special education teachers have discussed how much they have learned from each other as a result of co-teaching. Many of them make comments like this one I recently heard from a high school English teacher: "I was reluctant to co-teach because I wasn't sure of what teacher: "I was reluctant to co-teach because I wasn't sure of what it would be like. Now I can't believe I was concerned. I really don't ever want to go back to doing nothing but teaching by myself." A special educator said this: "Sometimes I want to apologize to all the students I taught in my special education classroom. I had no idea what general education is like. Co-teaching is a whole different world. It's been hard for me to adjust, but it's the best thing that ever happened for kids. I've learned so much from my teaching partner and together we're really making a difference." These comments indicate that co-teaching opens for educators a world of classroom collaboration and all the many added possibilities that it brings for teaching diverse groups of learners.

For Further Thought

1. How have you been personally affected by NCLB and IDEA? To what extent do you believe the changes you have experienced have been positive or negative? What is the basis for your thinking?

2. As you review research related to co-teaching, what does it suggest to you are the most critical elements of it? If you were to make one change in your own co-teaching on the basis of the research you reviewed, what would that change be?

3. Would you consider co-teaching a valid, research-based practice at this point in time? Why or why not? What other research do you think the field needs to clarify the impact of co-teaching on student outcomes?

4. How important are the traditional aspects of a rationale for co-teaching, those that originated in the early days of inclusive practices? How might you use information about the philosophical and anecdotal reasons for co-teaching to explain its importance to your administrator or a group of concerned parents?

Taking Action

1. With your colleagues, design a study that you could complete related to co-teaching at your school. You might use one of the studies reviewed in this chapter as a model, or you could design another type of action research project. Base your research on a critical question for which you believe an answer would improve co-teaching practices.

2. Have all the professionals in your school or at least those participating in co-teaching select articles to read from the bibliography in this chapter's appendix. Over several sessions or at department or faculty meetings, have individuals summarize what they have read and offer ideas about the implications of the information for their own classrooms and the school's program.

References

Barth, R. (2006). Improving relationships within the school house. *Educational Leadership, 63*(6), 8-13.

Bauwens, J., Hourcade, J. J., & Friend, M. (1989), Cooperative teaching: A model for general and special education integration. *Remedial and Special Education, 10*(2), 17-22.

Burnstein, N., Sears, S., Wilcoxen, A., Cabello, B., & Spagna, M. (2004). Moving toward inclusive practices. *Remedial and Special Education, 25*, 104-116.

Dunn, L. M. (1968). Special education for the mildly retarded-is much of it justifiable? *Exceptional Children, 35*, 5-22.

Epanchin, B. C., & Friend, M. (2007). The adolescence of inclusive practices: Building bridges through collaboration. In J. McLeskey (Ed.), *Classic articles about inclusion.* Arlington, VA: Council for Exceptional Children.

Garvar, A. G., & Papania, A. (1982). Team teaching: It works for the student. *Academic Therapy, 18*, 191-196.

Gerber, P., & Popp, A. (1999). Consumer perspectives on the collaborative teaching models: Views of students with and without LD and their parents. *Remedial and Special Education, 20*, 288-297.

Karger, J., & Hitchcock, C. (2003). *Access to the general curriculum for students with disabilities: a brief legal interpretation.* Wakefield, MA: National Center on Accessing the General Curriculum. Retrieved [insert date] from http://www.cast.org/publications/ncac/ncac_accesslegal.html.

Keefe, E. B., Moore, V., & Duff, F. (2004). The four "knows" of collaborative teaming. *Teaching Exceptional Children, 36*, 36-42.

Lortie, D. (1975). *Schoolteacher: A sociological study.* Chicago: University of Chicago Press.

Mastropieri, M. A., Scruggs, T. E., Graetz, J., Norland, J., Gardizi, W., & McDuffie, K. (2005). Case studies in co-teaching in the content areas: Successes, failures, and challenges. *Intervention in School and Clinic, 40*, 260-270.

Rea, P., McLaughlin, V. L., & Walther-Thomas, C. S. (2002). Outcomes for students with learning disabilities in inclusive and pullout programs. *Exceptional Children, 68*, 203-222.

Salisbury , C., & McGregor, G. (2002). The administrative climate and context of inclusive elementary schools. *Exceptional Children, 68*, 259-270.

Weiss, M. P., & Lloyd, J. (2003). Conditions for co-teaching: Lessons from a case study. *Teacher Education and Special Education, 26*, 27-41.

Will, M. C. (1986). Educating children with learning problems: A shared responsibility. *Exceptional Children, 53*, 411-415.

Wilson, G. L., & Michaels, C. A. (2006). General and special education students' perceptions of co-teaching: Implications for secondary-level literay instruction. *Reading & Writing Quarterly, 22*, 205-225.

Chapter 2 Appendix

• • • • • •

This appendix is a listing of many references and resources related to co-teaching. Some of the articles, chapters, and books have a research base, but others do not. The list also includes a separate section listing videotapes that describe co-teaching.

Selected Bibliography on Co-Teaching

Historical Perspectives

Adams, L., & Cessna, K. (1991). Designing systems to facilitate collaboration: Collective wisdom from Colorado. *Preventing School Failure, 35*(4), 37-42.

Adams, L., Tomlan, P., Cessna, K., & Friend, M. (1995). *Co-teaching: Lessons from practitioners.* Unpublished manuscript, Colorado Department of Education, Denver.

Armbruster, B., & Howe, C. E. (1985). Educators team up to help students learn. *NASSP Bulletin, 69*(479), 82-86.

Bauwens, J., Hourcade, J. J., & Friend, M. (1989). Cooperative teaching: A model for general and special education integration. *Remedial and Special Education, 10*(2), 17-22.

Epanchin, B. C., & Friend, M. (2008). The adolescence of inclusive practices: Building bridges through collaboration. In J. McLeskey (Ed.), *Classic articles about inclusion.* Arlington, VA: Council for Exceptional Children.

Friend, M., Reising, M., & Cook, L. (1993). Co-teaching: An overview of the past, a glimpse at the present, and considerations for the future. *Preventing School Failure, 37*(4), 6–10.

Garvar, A. G., & Papania, A. (1982). Team teaching: It works for the student. *Academic Therapy, 18,* 191-196.

Geen, A. G. (1985). Team teaching in the secondary schools of England and Wales. *Educational Review, 37,* 29–38.

Warwick, D. (1971). *Team teaching.* London: University of London.

Research on Co-Teaching

Appl, D. J., Troha, C., & Rowell, J. (2001). Reflections of a first-year team. *Teaching Exceptional Children, 33*(3), 4–8.

Austin, V. L. (2001). Teachers' beliefs about co-teaching. *Remedial and Special Education, 22,* 245–255.

Conderman, G., & Stephens, J. T. (2000). Reflections from beginning special educators. *Teaching Exceptional Children, 33*(1), 16–21.

daCosta, J. L., Marshall, J. L., & Riordan, G. (1998, April). *Case study of the development of a collaborative teaching culture in an inner city elementary school*. Paper presented at the annual meeting of the American Educational Research Association, San Diego, CA. (ERIC Documentation Reproduction Service No. ED420630)

Dieker, L. (2001). What are the characteristics of "effective" middle and high school co-taught teams for students with disabilities? *Preventing School Failure, 46,* 14-23.

Elbaum, B. (2002). The self-concept of students with learning disabilities: A meta-analysis of comparisons across different placements. *Learning Disabilities Research & Practice, 17,* 216-226.

Fennick, E., & Liddy, D. (2001). Responsibilities and preparation for collaborative teaching: Co-teachers' perspectives. *Teacher Education and Special Education, 24,* 229-240.

Foley, R. M. (2001). Professional development needs of secondary school principals of collaborative-based service delivery models. *High School Journal, 85*(1), 10-23.

Foley, R.M., & Mundschenk, N.A. (1997a). Collaboration activities and competencies of secondary school special educators: A national survey. *Teacher Education and Special Education, 20,* 47-60.

Foley, R.M., & Mundschenk, N.A. (1997b). Secondary school general educators' collaboration competencies and collaboration activities with general educators, special educators, and community service providers: A status report. *Journal of Research and Development in Education, 30,* 154-166.

Gerber, P., & Popp, A. (1999). Consumer perspectives on the collaborative teaching models: Views of students with and without LD and their parents. *Remedial and Special Education, 20,* 288-297.

Idol, L. (2006). Toward inclusion of special education students in general education: A program evaluation of eight schools. *Remedial and Special Education, 27,* 77-94.

Luckner, J. L. (1999). An examination of two co-teaching classrooms. *American Annals of the Deaf, 144,* 24–34.

Magiera, K., Smith, C., Zigmond, N., & Gebaner, K. (2005). Benefits of co-teaching in secondary mathematics classes. *Teaching Exceptional Children, 37*(3), 20-24.

Mastropieri, M. A., Scruggs, T. E., Graetz, J., Norland, J., Gardizi, W., & McDuffie, K. (2005). Case studies in co-teaching in the content areas: Successes, failures, and challenges. *Intervention in School and Clinic, 40*, 260-270.

Murawski, W., & Swanson, H. (2001). A meta-analysis of co-teaching research: Where are the data? *Remedial and Special Education, 22*, 258-267.

Murray, C. (2004). Clarifying collaborative roles in urban high schools: General educators' perspectives. *Teaching Exceptional Children, 36*(5), 44-51.

Rea, P., McLaughlin, V. L., & Walther-Thomas, C. S. (2002). Outcomes for students with learning disabilities in inclusive and pullout programs. *Exceptional Children, 68*, 203-222.

Salend, S. J., Johansen, M., Mumper, J., Chase, A. S., Pike, K. M., & Dorney, J. A. (1997). Cooperating teaching: The voices of two teachers. *Remedial and Special Education, 18*, 3-11.

Trent, S. C. (1998). False starts and other dilemmas of a secondary general education collaborative teacher. *Journal of Learning Disabilities, 31,* 503–513.

Wallace, T., Anderson, A. R., & Bartholomay, T. (2002). Collaboration: An element associated with the success of four inclusive high schools. *Journal of Educational and Psychological Consultation, 13*, 349-381.

Walther-Thomas, C. S. (1997). Co-teaching experiences: The benefits and problems that teachers and principals report over time. *Journal of Learning Disabilities, 30,* 395–407.

Wasburn-Moses, L. (2005). Roles and responsibilities of secondary special education teachers in an age of reform. *Remedial and Special Education, 26*, 151-158.

Weiss, M. P., & Lloyd, J. (2003). Conditions for co-teaching: Lessons from a case study. *Teacher Education and Special Education, 26*, 27-41.

Weiss, M. P., & Lloyd, J. W. (2002). Congruence between roles and actions of secondary special educators in co-taught and special education settings. *Journal of Special Education, 36*, 58-68.

Welch, M. (2000). Descriptive analysis of team teaching in two elementary classrooms: A formative experimental approach. *Remedial and Special Education, 21*, 366–376.

Wilson, G. L., & Michaels, C. A. (2006). General and special education students' perceptions of co-teaching: Implications for secondary-level literay instruction. *Reading and Writing Quarterly, 22*, 205-225.

Zigmond, N. (2006). Reading and writing in co-taught secondary school social studies classrooms: A reality check. *Reading and Writing Quarterly, 22*, 249-268.

Books and Other Resources

Basso, D., & McCoy, N. (2002). *The co-teaching manual.* Columbia, SC: Twins Publications.

Dieker, L. (2007). *Demystifying secondary inclusion: Powerful school-wide and classroom strategies.* Port Chester, NY: Dude Publishing.

Fishbaugh, M. S. E. (1997). *Models of collaboration.* Boston: Allyn & Bacon.

Fishbaugh, M. S. E. (2000). *The collaboration guide for early career educators.* Baltimore: Brookes.

Friend, M., Burrello, L., & Burrello, J. (2004). *Power of Two* (2nd edition) [videotape]. Bloomington, IN: Elephant Rock Productions, Indiana University, Forum on Education

Friend, M., & Bursuck, W. D. (2009). *Including students with special needs: A practical guide for classroom teachers* (5th edition). Boston: Allyn and Bacon.

Friend, M., & Cook, L. (2007). *Interactions: Collaboration skills for school professionals* (5th edition). Boston: Allyn and Bacon.

Hourcade, J., & Bauwens, J. (2002). *Cooperative teaching: Re-building and sharing the schoolhouse.* Austin, TX: Pro-Ed.

Villa, R. A., Thousand, J. S., & Nevin, A. I. (2004). *A guide to co-teaching: Practical tips for facilitating student learning.* Thousand Oaks, CA: Corwin.

Chapter 3
Co-Teaching Approaches

Quality is never an accident; it is always the result of high intention, sincere effort, intelligent direction and skillful execution; it represents the wise choice of many alternatives.

-New York Times Ad, 1939

Chapter Objectives

1. Describe six approaches for structuring co-taught classrooms, including examples, opportunities, challenges, and variations for each one.

2. List factors that may influence which approaches you select.

3. State ideas to keep in mind in order to make the best use of two professionals in the classroom.

Although successful co-teaching relies on many factors, perhaps the most essential dimension is the effective arrangement of the teachers and students so that learning is maximized. That is the focus of this chapter.

As you think about what a two-teacher classroom is like, keep in mind these points. First, co-teaching should be deliberate, that is, it should be designed based on an understanding of the content to be covered and the needs of students in the classroom (for example, Basso & McCoy, 2002; Bauwens & Hourcade, 2002; Villa, Thousand, & Nevin, 2004). Although all co-teachers occasionally have days in which one person runs into the classroom saying, "What are we doing today?," if this is the typical practice, it is unlikely the potential of co-teaching can be reached.

Second, part of the reason that co-teaching must be deliberate is because it is how students with disabilities receive the specialized instruction outlined on their individualized education programs (IEPs). Part of co-teaching should include opportunities for students to work on IEP goals, but that should occur, as much as possible, within the context of the overall instructional program. This topic is addressed further in Chapter 4.

Third, co-teaching presumes flexibility in terms of roles and responsibilities in the classroom. That is, sometimes the general educator is working with the large group and sometimes it is the special educator with that group. Sometimes both teachers are working with small groups. Remediation is not the sole responsibility of the special education teacher, and both teachers work with all the students in the class. They also share tasks such as discipline and classroom management.

Finally, co-teaching should always have the impact of *increasing instructional intensity.* A question co-teachers constantly ask themselves is this: How is this classroom providing more intense instruction than would have been possible with one teacher in the room? The implication is that both teachers are actively engaged in the teaching and learning process, so much so that their efforts have a significant positive impact on student achievement.

Six Co-Teaching Approaches

Co-teaching can be accomplished by arranging teachers and students using six specific approaches (Friend & Cook, 2007). These approaches are illustrated in Figure 3.1. Each one has advantages and drawbacks, and no single approach is considered to be the best one. You should think of these six approaches as a beginning since they do not at all represent the many variations creative co-teachers have invented in order to meet student needs. Similarly, you should not think of the approaches as existing in isolation. You might find that you use two or more approaches during a single lesson or that you blend the approaches to create new options. Finally, the goal is not to choose just one of these

Figure 3.1 Examples of Co-Teaching

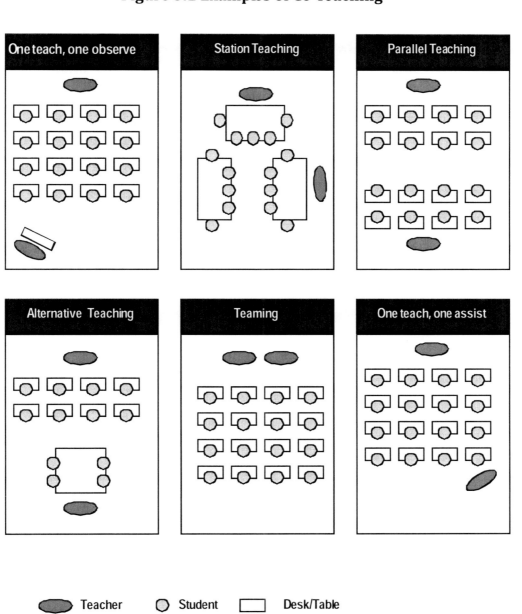

Teacher   Student   Desk/Table

Source: Figure 4.2 Co-Teaching Approaches from Friend, M., & Bursuck, W. D. (2009). *Including students with special needs: A practical guide for classroom teachers* (4th ed., p. 88). Boston: Allyn & Bacon. Copyright © 2002 by Pearson Education. Reprinted by permission of the publisher.

approaches; it is to use at least three and eventually all of these approaches to create the best learning opportunities for the students for whom you are responsible.

As you explore the co-teaching approaches, refer to the planning form included in this chapter's appendix. Use a lesson that you'll teach soon, and design alternative ways to present it using the co-teaching approaches.

One teaching, one observing

Recommended Use: Occasional

Decision-making in today's schools should be made based on data. Co-teaching gives educators a unique opportunity to gather important data that can then be used to improve student learning. In one teaching, one observing, one teacher manages the instruction of the entire student group while the other teacher systematically gathers data the two educators have decided are important. This approach generally should occur more frequently toward the end of the school year as teachers are learning about their students. It also should be used periodically as a concern arises (for example, several students are displaying increasingly disruptive behavior during class) or as teachers identify a specific type of information they need for decision-making (for example, assessment of sentence use during class discussion).

Many strategies are available to gather data in a co-taught classroom, and special educators usually have had one or more university course that directly address this topic. For example, they probably have learned how to complete an *ABC analysis,* which stands for antecedents-behaviors-consequences. This technique is helpful when teachers are trying to determine what is causing a particular behavior to occur. Another data collection strategy is event recording, where each time a behavior occurs it is noted. This strategy might be used to count how many times a student leaves his seat or calls out. Yet another observation technique is *interval recording.* In interval recording, a period of time is divided into twenty 30-second segments. The teacher observing simply marks whether the behavior under observation occurs during each of the segments. This technique might be used when the teachers suspect a student is frequently calling out during large-group instruction. Yet another strategy is *duration recording,* in which one teacher records how long a behavior occurs. This might be used to measure how long it takes certain students to begin assigned work or how long some students work before they become distracted.

These data collection ideas are just a few of the many that special educators have learned. These professionals also know that the specific approach to gathering observational data is determined by the goal for doing so, and they can help ensure that observing students results in valuable information that can be used to make classroom decisions.

One teaching, one observing in practice. Here are three examples of co-teachers using one teaching, one observing. Which recording strategy did the teachers use? How do you think they might change their instruction or classroom procedures based on the data they obtained?

- Two teachers are thinking that the school's intervention team should discuss a student struggling to learn. They decide to observe the student working individually in order to gain insight on what he does when he cannot answer a specific question, how long he works before becoming distracted, and who he asks for assistance from among his classmates.

- In a high school classroom, the teachers would like to know which students attempt to answer teacher questions during large group instruction. Using a seating chart, one teacher tallies which students raise their hands as questions are asked. The observer circles the tally of the student who was called on.

- In a middle school social studies class, the teachers frequently have students work in cooperative groups. They sense that some students are passive during these assignments, and they decide that the observer will spend two minutes watching each group to record which students initiate comments or questions and tally how many participate during each time interval.

Opportunities and challenges. Two teachers have the chance to focus on students in a way that that one teacher would never have the time to do, and so this co-teaching approach enables teachers to know subtleties about their students' learning needs. In some cases, though, the teachers may need to spend a few moments discussing what types of data would be helpful to have and how the data could be gathered. This is especially true in middle schools and high schools. When conducting professional development sessions on co-teaching with these professionals, they often comment that they have never collected data on their students. Another point of conversation might include deciding who should observe, including why it is important for both teachers to have opportunities to step back to formally observe students and use the information for making instructional decisions.

Variations on the approach. All of the examples provided thus far have focused on gathering data on students' academic, behavior, and social skills. A key variation of this approach shifts to looking at teachers' behaviors. Before describing this option, though, a caution is in order. Teachers in new partnerships probably should wait until they are comfortable with each other and their classroom practices before using this variation. In situations where any tension exists between the teachers, this variation is probably not a good idea to use because it might be viewed as evaluative of the teacher leading instruction.

All of that said, one teaching, one observing can be an invaluable way for teachers to monitor their own skills—outside a formal evaluation or mentoring process. For example, teachers might want to assess whether they call on boys and girls proportionately. They also might want to know whether they are asking various levels of questions of students and not just questions that tap basic comprehension. Another example concerns consistency in responding to student misbehavior. Does each teacher react in the same way, or does one have a stronger reaction than the other? What other teacher behaviors could you and a co-teacher decide to observe? How might data on those behaviors influence your co-teaching?

Station Teaching

Recommended Use: Frequent

In any material you read that discusses the topic of meeting the needs of diverse groups of learners, an always-recommended strategy is grouping students in various ways in order to better tailor instruction. This makes sense. Small groups can be arranged by skill level or by student interest. They can be based on mixing students at various learning levels or with different styles of social interaction. When co-teaching is in place, the options for using small groups become even greater.

In the basic station teaching approach, teachers divide the content to be addressed into three segments and then group students so that one-third begins with each part of the content. Each teacher works with a group and the third group works independently. During the lesson, the student groups rotate from station to station so that, by the end, all the students have completed all three and the teachers have each worked with every student in the class.

Elementary teachers are familiar with the concept of stations; many of these educators already use learning centers in their classrooms, and station teaching is a two-teacher variation of this practice. However, middle and high school teachers also should consider using stations, especially if they are in a block-scheduling arrangement.

Station teaching in practice. Here are examples of co-teaching using stations:

- In an elementary math class, students are learning about estimating. One group of students is estimating distance (for example, estimating how many footsteps it would take to walk around the perimeter of the classroom), one group is estimating repetitions (for example, how many times can you jump up and down in one minute), and one group is estimating with mass (for example, how many crayons will it take to balance the weights already on the scale). The first two groups are led by teachers; the third is independently completed by students working with a partner. During this 45-minute instructional period, all students will rotate to all three stations.

- In a high school U.S. history class (in a block schedule) , students are studying the industrial revolution. One group of students, led by a teacher, is discussing *The Jungle* by Upton Sinclair. A second group is reviewing material from the textbook with the other teacher. The third group is examining materials provided by the local historical society, including old photos depicting life at the beginning of the twentieth century. The students are discussing what life was like then and writing fictionalized life stories about the individuals portrayed in the photos.

Opportunities and challenges. Station teaching has many advantages. For example, by grouping students in various ways, teachers can more effectively reach instructional goals. For some activities, groups should be heterogeneous; for others, they could be skill-based. Station teaching also enables teachers to keep very close watch on student learning; with just eight or ten students in a group it is much easier than in the large group to see which students have understood the lesson and which need additional support. This co-teaching approach also lets teachers divide students who have behavior problems or difficulty working with each other. Finally, station teaching facilitates a highly interactive instructional environment. With multiple groups and multiple teachers, lessons can incorporate more student participation through discussion and activities.

However, station teaching also comes with some cautions. First, the activities that occur at each station must function independently of each other. If students must complete one station in order to do the next, this approach is not the one to use. For example, if teachers want students to pre-write, then draft an essay, and then edit the essay with their peers, station teaching is not appropriate—it would require that some students be assigned to edit before writing! If you review all the examples given, you'll see that each one meets this criterion. Each station can be successfully completed whether it is first, second, or third in the student's schedule.

Other cautions about station teaching concern logistics. Noise level can rise when small groups are used, and co-teachers may need to discuss how to keep everyone engaged but the noise level acceptable to both teachers and students. In addition, this co-teaching approach requires attention to timing. A planning task is to be sure the instruction and activities for each station require approximately the same amount of time. During the lesson, some co-teachers use a teach-timer that displays the time remaining for the station for both students and teachers.

Variations on the approach. The primary variations of station teaching concern changing the number of groups to suit the co-teaching situation. For example, in a middle or high school with traditional as opposed to block schedules (Weller & McLeskey, 2000), three stations in a class period may not be feasible. In that case, the teachers might plan just two stations, eliminating the independent station. Further, the teachers could decide that when it is time to change stations, the teachers can move instead of the students, thus saving valuable instructional time. Another option for secondary educators in traditionally-scheduled schools is to use station teaching as part of a two-day lesson plan. During the first part of the first day, the teachers might team. During the second half of that period, students complete the first of three stations. When they return the next day, they complete the two remaining stations. In high schools, teachers occasionally extend this thinking further by planning a three-day lesson in which students remain in a single station for an entire class period.

Parallel Teaching

Recommended Use: Frequent

Are you the type of person who tends to be most comfortable when you can blend in with a large group? Are you uncomfortable when you are called upon to answer a question or take a leadership role or when everyone turns to listen to your opinion? As an adult, your preference is just that—a preference. However, some students feel this same way—and if they do not call attention to themselves they sometimes cruise through their education, perhaps not achieving in the way they would if they received more individualized attention. Parallel teaching is a co-teaching approach that permits teachers to provide that attention.

In the most basic version of parallel teaching, the professionals divide students into two groups and lead the same instruction with both groups. That is, they may both address the math objective for the day by introducing students to finding the volume of a prism, or they may both conduct a review session for the unit exam to be given the next day. In this co-teaching approach, students receive instruction from one of the teachers, but not both; the groups do not rotate.

Parallel teaching in practice. Here are examples of parallel teaching as implemented by experienced co-teachers:

- In a sixth grade English/language arts class the students are reading *Bridge to Terabithia* by Katherine Paterson. They have read the first four chapters, and it is time for discussion to check comprehension and also to consider the themes of the novel. The teachers divide the students into two heterogeneous groups, paying attention to which students tend to have lots to say during discussions and which tend to be quiet. Once divided, each teacher discusses with students Jess and Leslie's friendship, using these questions:

  - Do you think Jess and Leslie's friendship is believable? Why or why not?
  - Have you ever been friends with someone who is different than you? How were you different? Did this make your friendship easier or harder? Why?
  - How do your friends help you see things in a different way?

  By having the discussions running concurrently, each student has the opportunity to discuss their own experiences with friendships, and the teachers can ensure that even students usually reluctant to participate can do so.

- The objectives for students in a chemistry class are to

  - Distinguish between chemical reactions that are reversible and those that go to completion.
  - Explain the concept of chemical equilibrium.
  - Understand how Le Chatelier's Principle works on a chemical reaction at equilibrium.

In a large group, the students have observed and participated in several demonstrations of reversible chemical reactions (for example, hot wheels cars that change color with temperature), those that go to completion (for example, burning a match), and chemical equilibrium (for example, NO_2-N_2O_4 gas tubes in both cold and hot water). The teachers then divide the students into two groups to discuss what they have observed and to generate examples from everyday life that demonstrate chemical equilibrium. Each group produces a chart of their responses, and they are posted so everyone in class can see them; homework for students is to design a controlled paper wad fight that would demonstrate the principle of equilibrium.

Opportunities and challenges. The opportunities and challenges of parallel teaching are very similar to those of station teaching. That is, this co-teaching approach permits teachers to assign students to groups to maximize student participation and minimize behavior problems. It increases the number of times that each student can respond during teacher-led instruction, and increases instructional intensity by ensuring that each teacher has an active role in the classroom.

Potential challenges in parallel teaching include these: First, this approach is only effective if the teachers can offer equivalent instruction to students. If one teacher is unsure of the material being taught, the students she works with would be at a disadvantage during a learning assessment. This often implies that if the special educator is not highly qualified in the content area in which co-teaching is occurring, parallel teaching is reserved mostly as a technique for review.

Second, this approach requires that teachers take about the same amount of time to complete instruction, and teachers have to learn to pace instruction accordingly. Third, noise level can be significant during parallel teaching, and teachers may need to discuss their tolerance for noise as well as that of the students.

Variations on the approach. Parallel teaching is a flexible means for enhancing instruction. For example, it can be used when students are at two different skill levels, especially for elementary students.

In a math class, the teachers together discussed and demonstrated multiplication. After the lesson, the students were divided into two groups based on their level of understanding. One group worked on multiplication problems using manipulatives while the other did the same problems without manipulatives.

Another use for parallel teaching is to present different points of view on a single topic. Two teachers introduce the causes of the Civil War by having one group learn about the perspective of the states that seceded from the Union, emphasizing their perception of the "War of Northern Aggression." The other group learns about the issues of slavery and human rights. After the two groups complete their lesson, they join for a whole-class debate. Notice how this application of parallel teaching could be used in any instruction where the goal was to help students understand multiple points of view (for example, characters' perspectives a piece off literature taught in English or language arts, scientific debates).

Alternative Teaching

Recommended Use: Occasional

Co-teachers often are able to notice their students' needs in a way that one teacher cannot. They may find that some students have quickly mastered certain concepts and might benefit from enrichment, or they may note that some students struggling with the content would benefit from additional direct instruction. Similarly, they may realize that several students share a particular interest or that a few students are better able to focus when they work in a small group led by one of the teachers.

All of the implied instructional needs in these examples could easily be met using alternative teaching. In this approach, one teacher manages the large group while the other takes a small group for a specific instructional purpose. This small group might meet for a few minutes while other students check homework or complete a warm-up task, or it might meet after initial instruction occurs. In elementary schools, the small group could meet either later or earlier in the day.

Alternative teaching in practice. These examples of alternative teaching are designed to demonstrate the wide variety of instructional needs it can address:

- Two elementary teachers know they have several students who would benefit from pre-teaching. Before they begin the unit on land formations, they decide to pull a group to introduce the new vocabulary. Among the students in the group are Simon, a student with a significant learning disability in the area of reading; Mitchell, a student who takes medication for ADHD; Charity, a student who is uncertain of herself and tends to avoid participating in a group unless she is sure she knows the answer; and Maria, an English language learner who struggles with her schoolwork. The general education teacher completes a mini-lesson on the vocabulary (for example, plain, mesa, isthmus, peninsula) while the special education teacher finishes helping students put away materials from their writing project and prepare for social studies.

- In 7th grade math, the co-teachers have completed a two-day lesson that addresses these objectives:

  - Identify and apply properties of real numbers, including pi.

  - Select and apply instruments (including rulers) and units of measure to the degree of accuracy required.

  - Use concrete and graphic representations and applicable formulae to find the perimeter of two-dimensional figures.

  The students have measured several round objects in the room (for example, a coffee can) to determine perimeter and circumference. They then divide the circumference by the diameter and learn that this number approximates pi. During the second day, while some students independently complete a worksheet extending this concept, the general education teacher works with six students who do not yet seem to understand the concept. They measure additional objects, complete the division, and compare their answers to pi.

Opportunities and challenges. Many co-teachers worry that students with disabilities may not receive the individual attention they need in a large class group. Alternative teaching permits teachers to provide those intense, small-group sessions within the context of the classroom. This co-teaching approach also can provide instructional flexibility. That is, teachers can use it to provide enrichment, remediation, assessment, or pre-teaching. Alternative teaching also can enable teachers to have more personalized interactions with students.

The most obvious challenge to this co-teaching approach is preventing the small group from being seen as the equivalent of a pullout special education classroom in the corner of the room. If students perceive that classmates with IEPs are repeatedly identified to participate in the small group, the core co-teaching concept of seamless education without stigma is violated.

To avoid this problem, co-teachers can use several strategies. First, they can vary who is leading instruction for the small group. If the general education teacher sometimes works with the group needing remediation, less stigma may occur. Second, the teachers can clearly vary the purposes of the group, making sure they use alternative teaching for at least three different instructional purposes. Finally, using a class roster and a form like the one included in the appendix at the end of this chapter, co-teachers can keep a record of which students have been pulled for small-group work so they can track to be sure all students are occasionally put into the small group and no student is in the small group every time this approach is employed.

Variations on the approach. The examples provided thus far were set in the context of academic instruction. However, alternative teaching can be effective for managing student behavior as well. For example, if one or two students tend to be disruptive and, despite teachers' best efforts, are interfering with the progress of classmates, the co-teachers might decide to spend a couple of days with those two students in a small group that also includes two positive role models and a student who just transferred to the district. The teacher working with the small group follows the same lesson plan as the teacher leading the large group. By placing the students with behavior concerns in a small group closely supervised by one teacher, their learning can be focused and the rest of the class can learn as well.

Teaming

Recommended Use: Occasional

Some teachers describe co-teaching as having "one brain in two bodies." They refer to finishing each other's sentences and to the wonderful choreography of a two-teacher classroom. These teachers generally are discussing teaming.

In teaming, both teachers are in front of the classroom, sharing the responsibility of leading instruction, as when the kindergarten co-teachers together instruct children about their community. Alternatively, co-teachers may have different but equally active roles, as when one teacher leads a large-group lesson while the other teacher models note-taking on the overhead projector. The key characteristic of this co-teaching approach is that both teachers are fully engaged in the delivery of the core instruction.

Teaming in practice. Co-teachers frequently use teaming at all grade levels and across all subject areas. Here are two examples:

• In algebra, co-teachers are working with students on the concepts of lines and slopes. The day's lesson includes writing an equation for a line already known. After reviewing how to graph a line, how to determine slope, and how to determine whether lines intercept, the students are being introduced to writing an equation for a line already known. At the beginning of this lesson, the special education teacher leads during the review and the general education teacher demonstrates the concepts using graphs that have been loaded for use on the smartboard, interjecting clarifying questions. When the new concept is introduced, the general education teacher takes more of a lead while the special educator moves to the smartboard, working examples and interjecting questions as the general education teacher had done during the first part of the lesson.

- In a second grade classroom, the teachers have used the book *How Big Is a Foot?* by Rolf Myller as part of a unit on linear measure. In the story, the bed ordered for the queen's birthday ends up being too short because the order was placed based on the length of the king's long feet, but it was made by the craftsman whose feet were much shorter. The point for students is that measures are consistent so that results are reliable. The teachers come to class the day of the lesson wearing different shoes: One has on brightly colored shoes, but they are just her typical size. The other has on a pair of her son's size 17 sneakers. The teachers demonstrate the difference in "six feet" when shoe size is the measure and introduce the ruler, comparing it to each of the shoes. After the teachers encourage the children to estimate how many non-standard and standard feet are in several examples of taped lines they have put on the floor of the classroom, the students all trace their own shoes, cut them out, compare them to a standard foot (the ruler), measure several additional items, and then write a paragraph to reflect on their learning.

Opportunities and challenges. Teaming can be very energizing. Some teachers comment that working with a partner they are willing to try new ways to reach students they never would have tried if teaching alone. They also can increase the entertainment factor of teaching; through instructional conversations, sharing question-asking, and the antics that sometimes are part of this co-teaching approach, students are more likely to remain attentive.

As with all co-teaching approaches, however, this one also has some challenges. You may have been surprised that this approach is recommended for occasional rather than frequent use. That is because this approach loses the valuable instructional technique of grouping. When both teachers are in front of the class, they may not be as aware of the individual and subtle needs of their students.

A second challenge of teaming relates to the comfort level of teachers. If you and your co-teacher have just begun your partnership or are just not very comfortable working together in the classroom, this approach may call for more flexibility than can reasonably be expected. That is, some co-teachers may use this approach intuitively and almost as soon as they begin co-teaching, some may use it once they learn each other's styles and develop instructional trust, and some may find teaming just is not an approach they can implement.

Finally, if both partners tend to talk quite a bit, teaming can be challenging. One teacher may provide an example, which prompts the other teacher to give another example, which prompts the first teacher to relate a real life experience, and so on. Co-teachers may have to gauge their contributions so that pacing is maintained.

Variations on the approach. Teaming can bring out the creative side of teachers. When elementary teaching partners were introducing the concepts of vertical and horizontal, one teacher wore a blouse with vertical stripes while the other wore a shirt with horizontal stripes. They each explained the concept their clothing was illustrating. Two high school teachers in a civics and government class debated whether a woman should be president. They then asked students to write a reflective essay that distinguished between the facts and opinions the teachers had demonstrated. The next day the students engaged in debates of interest to them. In a middle school science class, one teacher usually gives directions for the lab while the other demonstrates the directions, quizzing students, occasionally making intentional mistakes to check student comprehension, and asking the students to repeat directions to confirm understanding.

Overall, teaming is an option for partners to bring to the instructional situation what each has as a first area of expertise, as discussed in Chapter 1—core content for the general education teachers and learning process for the special education teachers.

One Teaching, One Assisting

Recommended Use: Seldom

The final co-teaching approach places one teacher in a lead role while the other clearly is functioning as a support to the classroom. In this approach, one teacher leads the instruction while the other monitors student work, addresses behavior issues, answers student questions, and facilitates instruction by distributing papers or other materials. The teacher who is assisting might sometimes ask the leading teacher a question to clarify a concept or direction he has noticed is a problem for the students. In some ways, one teaching, one assisting frequently serves as a type of informal observation.

One teaching, one assisting in practice. One teaching, one assisting can be helpful in certain types of instructional situations. Here are two examples:

• In biology, students are learning about chromatography as a means to separate mixtures. Objectives include these:

  • Perform a paper chromatography separation of pigment mixture and analyze its separate parts by determining the R_f (retention factor).
  • Using leaf chromatography, show that the R_f is a constant.

The students have experimented using grape Kool-aid and water-based markers. As they begin to use crushed fresh leaves in a solution, a procedure that calls for patience on the part of students and careful attention to detail. As the filter paper is dipped into the leaf and solvent mixture, one teacher continues to provide instruction and directions while the other moves around the classroom, checking to be sure each student is completing the experiment correctly.

• The fifth grade class is reviewing long division. One teacher writes a problem on the board, and the students all solve it using individual whiteboards and markers. At the other teacher's signal, they all hold up their whiteboards, and the assisting teacher checks to be sure that all the students have completed the problem correctly.

Opportunities and challenges. The opportunities related to one teaching, one assisting generally relate to the provision of individual and classroom support. An example of individual support comes from high schools, where some students have noted that they like having the option of quietly signaling the assisting teacher to have a quick question answered or word defined. It is less embarrassing than raising their hands and asking their questions in front of the whole class. Classroom support has already been illustrated: By having one teacher check student responses and carry out management tasks such as distributing materials, instruction can be effective and efficient.

Of all the co-teaching approaches, however, one teaching, one assisting has the greatest potential to be over-used and abused. In fact, this approach to co-teaching is the one that co-teaching supervisors and observers worry about most. In too many classrooms, the general education teacher continues to teach as she did in a one-teacher class while the special educator works either as a passive partner who waits for instruction to finish before helping students who struggle to learn or as a highly paid teaching assistant. Even if the teachers reverse roles occasionally (although when this approach is used too frequently, that generally is not the case), the problem is not diminished. The classroom still has just one teacher, thus eliminating the entire wealth of instructional possibilities that would otherwise be possible.

Some teachers indicate that they use this approach to help students attend to instruction. However, when a teacher stops to talk to a student, it is as likely that he will completely shift the student's attention rather than focusing it. Other teachers say this is their primary approach because the special education teacher is not familiar with the core curriculum. If that is the case, the teachers should discuss other options for co-teaching, at least occasionally, so that partnership can grow. Yet other teachers use this approach because they lack planning time. That topic will be addressed in Chapter 5, but it is not an excuse for over-using one teaching, one assisting.

Ultimately, comments made to special educators by students in classrooms where this approach is too common illustrate its dangers:

* *Do they pay you to do this?*
* *Are they ever going to let you have your own classroom?*
* *I don't have to listen to you. You're not the real teacher.*

Variations on the approach. So many cautions should be kept in mind about one teaching, one assisting that mentioning variations on the approach seems to raise the likelihood that it will be used inappropriately, and so perhaps one additional point of emphasis should be made instead. If this approach is used, both teachers should have opportunities to take on both roles, and they should deliberately ensure that they both work with all the students in the class so that no stigma results from any student-teacher interaction.

Selecting Co-Teaching Approaches

The six co-teaching approaches provide a framework for thinking about what a co-taught class should look like. However, co-teachers may find that they use certain approaches more than others and that they have questions about implementing them.

Factors That May Influence Co-Teaching

Several suggestions can be given regarding selecting co-teaching approaches. How does each of these areas affect your thinking about using the co-teaching approaches?

Student characteristics and needs. As you might guess, students are the first consideration in selecting co-teaching approaches. For example, if your students easily handle transitions between activities and generally are focused on instruction, you probably can use any of the approaches that have been described. However, if your students are easily distracted or tend to become disruptive during transitions, you might choose approaches with less student movement such as parallel teaching or teaming. Here are other examples of student characteristics that might affect your selection of approaches—and you probably can think of others:

- Student need for structure and predictability

- Student attentional skills

- Diversity of student learning levels represented in the class

- Physical or sensory needs of students (for example, need for an interpreter, need for wheelchair access to all parts of the room)

- Student use of assistive technology (for example, need for a communication board or computer access)

Teacher considerations. You and your teaching partner represent a second factor that affects the selection of approaches. For example, if you and your co-teacher both are new at this service delivery option, you might begin with mostly parallel or station teaching with just a little use of one teaching and one assisting (both teachers taking on both roles, of course). This combination of approaches establishes clearly that two teachers are present in the classroom, avoids the risk of recreating a pullout remedial program that could occur with alternative teaching, and provides immediate benefit to students who benefit from increased instructional intensity. Two teachers who have co-taught before might make different selections based on their experiences.

Sometimes one teacher is more comfortable with the idea of a two-teacher classroom than the other, regardless of their co-teaching history. In these situations, the teachers might decide that the first four weeks of the partnership will be spent primarily in observing and assisting while their relationship develops, but they then should move beyond the beginner stage. A similar approach to developing effective classroom practices might also be needed if the special educator in a middle or high school does not have the content knowledge necessary to take a lead role in the class. For example, Jamie, a special educator who co-teaches geometry with Chris, a math teacher with 12 years of experience, may feel intimidated. Jamie may not have studied geometry since her own high school days, and she may fear making mistakes and causing Chris to have to take over or correct her. The same gradual approach of building a classroom partnership is in order. What is not acceptable is for the teacher to decide that for the entire first year Jamie should mostly assist in order to learn the curriculum. While the second co-teaching year for these professionals undoubtedly will be richer and more comfortable than the first, they should actively work to gradually increase Jamie's participation throughout the first year. Said directly, professionals are not entitled to a year's salary for learning the middle school or high school curriculum.

One other factor for teachers to keep in mind as they co-teach is relative to the experience of the teachers and the effect it may have on structuring co-taught lessons. Think about these combinations: two novice or early career teachers, two veteran teachers, one novice teacher and one experienced teacher. What strengths might each of these combinations of professional have? What concerns might result just because of their experience levels?

Features of the curriculum. Although creative teachers are constantly finding ways to use all the co-teaching approaches at all levels and across all academic subject matter, teachers might find, especially at the beginning, that their subject matter makes certain approaches more attractive than others. For example, in elementary reading programs in which students are grouped by their skill levels, station teaching is likely to be frequently used. In middle school math, teachers may find that they can ensure student understanding and check student work for accuracy most efficiently by using parallel teaching. In a high school civics and government class, though, the teachers may find that teaming is often appropriate when combined with alternative teaching for work on special projects. The point of thinking about curriculum is this: When co-teaching is a new endeavor, use structures that most easily match the curriculum. As the partnership grows, try to expand the number of approaches used in order to increase instructional intensity.

Pragmatic issues. Two concerns about using the co-teaching approaches often arise: time for planning and space limitations resulting from crowded classrooms. Finding time for shared planning is addressed in detail in Chapter 5. Here, a specific bit of advice can be offered. If teachers have limited or non-existent planning time, they should consider basing their co-teaching on the patterns that occur in instruction. If certain lessons tend to involve introducing a lot of vocabulary, the teachers might use station teaching whenever those lessons occur. When a unit is being reviewed, they might decide generally to select parallel teaching. During the weekly review on Fridays, alternative teaching may be the approach of choice. That is, when planning time is limited, finding efficient ways to structure the classroom can make effective co-teaching more feasible.

Space sometimes is a serious concern for co-teachers. A spacious classroom does make using the six approaches more feasible, but even in a crowded classroom you should experiment with several student grouping strategies. For example, in parallel, station, or alternative teaching, you might have the teachers move to work with different student groups instead of having the students move. In elementary and middle schools, you also could have one group of students seated closely together on the floor while the other group works at desks. Another option is to use all the approaches but to be sure that classroom furniture is arranged to accommodate them before the lesson begins.

Additional Considerations

In observing co-teachers and interacting with them in all types of schools in all parts of the country, several other topics are mentioned often enough that they should be noted here.

Non-Approaches A few teachers somehow arrive at the decision that co-teaching means they take turns. One way they decide to take turns is to alternate weeks (or units or chapters) in terms or planning and leading instruction. Dividing teaching in this way undermines the entire point of co-teaching—it doesn't draw on the strengths that each professional brings to the situation. Another example of taking turns may occur even if the teachers jointly plan instruction. They may say, "I lead on Mondays and he leads on Tuesdays. That way we're sure we both teach." Comments such as these usually suggest that the teachers have not embraced the collaborative dimension of co-teaching and are at a very early stage in the development of their practices. In both types of turn-taking, the fundamental issue becomes one of the value of having two teachers in the classroom. If turns are taken, the situation looks remarkably like job sharing instead of co-teaching.

Tailoring Approaches to Your Situation As you experiment with the co-teaching approaches, you'll probably discover that you sometimes blend two or more approaches in a single lesson, create your own variations of them, and develop your own signature for co-teaching structures. As this happens, you should congratulate yourselves—this means your understanding of co-teaching and its power is maturing and becoming integral to instruction. The six approaches truly are intended to be just a starting point, a way of discussing co-teaching that permits clear explanations and options for painting verbal pictures of co-taught classrooms. They are the basis for moving to a new level that can be uniquely yours.

Rethinking Common Teacher Practices Some professionals may find that co-teaching causes them to rethink some of the habits they have developed as effective teachers. For example, when working with a small group of students, most teachers sit so that they face the classroom in order to ensure that other students are working. In co-teaching, however, when two teachers are simultaneously working with student groups, they may find it is better to position themselves parallel to each other (that is, both with their backs to the same wall) or back-to-back (that is, toward the center of the classroom so their voices are directed to a wall). The latter two options help the teachers from talking over each other and distracting students.

Another common positive teaching habit is to stand while delivering instruction. In co-taught classes, though, often it is important for the teachers—even if working with half the students—to reduce the teacher voice carryover by sitting at a desk or on a chair with the students clustered around it. What are other teacher habits that might have to be reconsidered in the context of a co-teaching program?

When you teach, do you often use choral responding to increase student participation? That's a great idea and can be effective in co-taught classes during teaming or other large group activities. However, when students are in small groups it can be distracting. An alternative is to have available for each student a personal white board or slate on which answers can be written and then displayed. What other nonverbal strategies could you use during co-teaching to address noise level while keeping students actively participating?

For Further Thought

1. As you think about the co-teaching in which you participate or are planning, which approaches seem most suited to your situation? What does your co-teacher think?

2. Which approach have you used least in your co-teaching? How could you use this approach (either alone or blended with

others) in an upcoming lesson?

3. What factors may influence your decisions about co-teaching approaches? Why? How do your perceptions compare with those of your co-teacher?

4. How can you avoid or reduce the problem of too much use of one teaching, one assisting? What plans could you and your co-teacher make to address this topic?

Taking Action

1. Conduct an anonymous survey of all the co-teaching partners in your school using the form included in the appendix for this chapter. What do the results tell you about use of the co-teaching approaches in your school? Have a co-teaching brainstorming session to generate new ideas for expanding the use of the co-teaching approaches that can have the greatest impact on student learning.

2. Plan for exchange visits among co-teachers. If your school has an extensive co-teaching program, arrange for novices to observe in veterans' classrooms. If your program is relatively new, perhaps you could arrange to visit co-taught classrooms in a neighboring school or district.

References

Basso, D., & McCoy, N. (2002). *The co-teaching manual.* Columbia, SC: Twins Publications.

Bauwens, J., & Hourcade. J. J. (2002). *Cooperative teaching: Rebuilding the schoolhouse for all students* (2nd edition). Austin, TX: Pro-Ed.

Friend, M., & Cook, L. (2007). *Interactions: Collaboration skills for school professionals* (5th edition). Boston: Allyn and Bacon.

Villa, R. A., Thousand, J. S., & Nevin, A. I. (2004). *A guide to co-teaching: Practical tips for facilitating student learning.* Thousand Oaks, CA: Corwin.

Weller, D. R., & McLeskey, J. (2000). Block scheduling and inclusion in a high school: Teacher perceptions of the benefits and challenges. *Remedial and Special Education, 21*, 209-218.

CHAPTER 3 APPENDIX

• • • • • •

The forms included on the following pages were referenced in Chapter 3. They are included in the order in which they were mentioned in the chapter and are intended to assist you in thinking about co-teaching approaches and applying them to your co-teaching situation.

Tracking Students Participation in the Small Group during Alternative Teaching

This form enables co-teachers to keep track over time of which students have been in a small group and for what purpose.

Student Name	Date and Purpose of the Small Group									

From Isolation to Partnership: Applying Co-Teaching Approaches

You are accustomed to thinking about teaching as an endeavor in which one person leads. If you are a veteran teacher, you probably have many ideas and patterns that you use to be an effective teacher. As you read about the co-teaching approaches, use this form to re-design a specific lesson to incorporate each approach. Complete each section for a one-teacher lesson and then jot options for changing the lesson plan to take advantage of the talents of two teachers.

Subject _____ Topic/Lesson _____Date _____

Competencies/Objectives

_____
_____
_____
_____

Materials

_____
_____
_____
_____

Special Student Needs

_____
_____
_____
_____

	One Teacher Lesson	Co-Taught Lesson Approach _____
Anticipatory Set		
Procedures		
Independent practice		
Closure		
Assessment		
Accommodations and modifications for students with disabilities or other special needs		
Notes		

Survey on Co-Teaching Approaches

Use this survey to have co-teachers estimate the proportion of their shared time they use each approach. What do the results suggest in terms of areas for discussion and growth?

Actual% **Ideal %**

_____ _____ **One Teach, One Observe.** In this co-teaching approach more detailed observation of students engaged in the learning process can occur. With this approach co-teachers can decide in advance what types of specific observational information to gather during instruction and can agree on a system for gathering the data. Afterward, the teachers should analyze the information together.

_____ _____ **Station Teaching.** In this co-teaching approach, teachers divide content and students. Each teacher then teaches the content to one group and subsequently repeats the instruction for the other group. If appropriate, a third "station" could give students an opportunity to work independently.

_____ _____ **Parallel Teaching.** On occasion, students' learning would be greatly facilitated if they just had more supervision by the teacher or more opportunity to respond. In parallel teaching, the teachers are both teaching the same information, but they divide the class group and do so simultaneously.

_____ _____ **Alternative Teaching:** In most class groups, occasions arise in which several students need specialized attention. In alternative teaching, one teacher takes responsibility for the large group while the other works with a smaller group.

_____ _____ **Teaming:** In teaming, both teachers are delivering the same instruction at the same time. Some teachers refer to this as having "one brain in two bodies." Others call it "tag team teaching." Most co-teachers consider this approach the most complex but satisfying way to co-teach, but it is the approach that is most dependent on teachers' styles.

_____ _____ **One Teaching, One Assisting.** In this approach to co-teaching, one person would keep primary responsibility for teaching while the other professional circulates through the room providing unobtrusive assistance to students as needed.

100% **100%** **TOTAL**

If you'd like to make additional comments about co-teaching approaches in our school, please use the reverse side. Thanks for participating.

Chapter 4
Classroom Matters for Co-Teaching
● ● ● ● ● ●

> *If you have an apple and I have an apple and we exchange*
> *these apples then you and I will still each have one apple.*
> *But if you have an idea and I have an idea and we exchange*
> *these ideas, then each of us will have two ideas.*

> **— George Bernard Shaw**

Chapter Objectives

1. Analyze topics that co-teachers should address in order to strengthen their partnership and avoid miscommunication.

2. Discuss topics related to classroom and behavior management that co-teachers may need to negotiate.

3. Incorporate effective instructional practices and student evaluation strategies into co-teaching.

Understanding the many different ways that co-teachers can arrange themselves and students in order to maximize learning is just the first step to designing and sustaining a co-teaching program. As you experiment with co-teaching approaches, it is also important that you address other dimensions of co-teaching. First, co-teachers need to nurture their working relationship (Dieker, 2001; Gately & Gately, 2001). Perhaps because teaching traditionally has been an occupation of isolation, even professionals who are friends outside the classroom sometimes have to work diligently to create a strong partnership inside the classroom.

●
●
●
●
●

Second, co-teachers usually find they have to discuss various classroom and behavior management issues. They may share similar perspectives on some aspects of setting up and efficiently managing a shared class, but they may differ on others. Finally, co-teaching by itself is not likely to provide meaningful access to curriculum and improve outcomes for students unless exemplary instructional practices are put in place (Abell, Bauder, & Simmons, 2005; Lawrence-Brown, 2004).

Some of the topics addressed in this chapter may be inconsequential for you and your co-teacher. Others may be significant. One point this chapter makes is that, just like in a marriage, clear communication is essential. Co-teachers may chuckle to think others worry about some of the matters raised here, but they also may find some of these topics are ones that they have found bothersome. Discussing areas of concern soon after they are noticed can prevent small disagreements from becoming serious problems that interfere with co-teaching effectiveness.

In the appendix that follows this chapter, you will find the *Colorado Assessment of Co-Teaching* (Co-ACT), a research-based instrument that can assist you in reflecting on your current co-teaching practices and those you consider ideal. It functions as a summary of much of the information presented in this chapter. It is most useful as a tool for discussing the topics it addresses and is not intended as an evaluation instrument.

Strengthening the Co-Teaching Partnership

Some co-teachers find that co-teaching is exactly what they have always wanted to do. They happily work with their colleague and respond to their diverse students' needs, and few dilemmas occur. However, this is not always the case. When it is not, many of the concerns reported by co-teachers are not about students with disabilities or instructional matters. Instead, professionals express concerns about their working relationships with co-teachers (Murray, 2004; Wasburn-Moses, 2005). Some general educators would like special education teachers to take more responsibility in the classroom and are frustrated that they do not. Some special educators would like to provide assistance to students during instruction and are concerned that they are asked to refrain from walking around the room as initial instruction is offered by the general education teacher.

These examples only begin to illustrate the complexity of a two-teacher classroom and the importance of highly developed communication skills, the ability to negotiate, and the commitment to raise areas of frustration so they can be resolved (Hourcade & Bauwens, 2002). In this section, some of the topics that co-teachers might need to discuss are briefly outlined. Many of them will not be a concern for you and your partner, but others may lead to spirited discussions about ways to implement co-teaching. You probably can find additional topics that are important, and I hope that you add those to your list.

Parity in the Classroom

How will you communicate to each other, to students, and to parents that you and your teaching partner have equivalent expertise and truly share responsibility in the classroom? This topic relates to the description of collaboration presented in Chapter 1. At the elementary level, parity may relate to who begins instruction or gives permission for students to leave the classroom. In middle and high school, parity may be directly related to who stands at the front of the classroom during instruction and who grades student work. Remember that special and general education teachers have different types of expertise. The goal is to find ways to blend them to enhance student learning (Murray, 2004). Some common and essential indicators of parity are included in a checklist in the appendix that follows this chapter, and attention to them can enhance your partnership. Are there others that you would add?

Division of Labor for Teaching and Related Responsibilities

In some schools, general education teachers express concern that special educators go from room to room without any specific obligations to be active participants in the teaching process and all the many tasks it requires. Although it is not reasonable to expect special educators who co-teach in several classes to share half the teaching tasks in each one, co-teachers should discuss which teaching responsibilities could be shared or how the preparation of materials could be divided.

Preferences for Out-of-Class Communication

Co-teachers who spend the day together have ongoing opportunities to discuss their instruction and students. However, in a large school in which co-teachers may not see each other except during their co-teaching time, they may need to discuss their preferred communication options. For example, e-mail may be viewed as the optimum strategy because it can be stored on a computer. A few teachers, though, do not regularly access e-mail and prefer a face-to-face meeting after school or a phone call in the evening.

Strategies for Responding to Mistakes that Occur During Teaching

Have you ever realized that you made a serious error in your teaching or had your students point out that you had made a mistake? Perhaps when adding 29 and 48 you wrote 67 on the board. Or you may have misspelled the word perseverance as *perserverence.* You quickly corrected it and moved on because errors are part of teaching. However, teachers sometimes worry about how to respectfully tell their co-teacher during the teaching process about an error, especially when special educators are teaching in an area in which they have limited experience or general educators tend to retain most of the ownership for instruction. This topic can easily be addressed before the problem arises. Some teachers might agree that the person who notices the mistake will just correct it without saying anything. Others might want to use signal words in a class. They agree that if one person says, "I'd like to rephrase that," it means there has been an error that needs correcting. The specific strategy for addressing is not the issue—it's having a respectful way to do so that has been decided upon in advance.

Preferences for Receiving Feedback

Most professionals are self-aware, knowing that they respond best when they receive feedback in a certain manner. Perhaps they want to be sure that any debriefing occurs the same day as a lesson, or perhaps they would like to wait until the next day to discuss anything that occurred. Most professionals would prefer that any discussion about a disagreement on teaching procedures, responses to students, or other topics be completed in private (not the teacher's lounge) and with respect. You may find that you never need to follow the strategy you and your colleague develop for exchanging feedback, but if a need arises the plan is in place. One difficult aspect of co-teaching for some professionals is opening discussion of topics where disagreement exists. One teacher might use cynicism in talking to students and it bothers the other teacher. One teacher may not consistently implement the classroom behavior management plan, and this frustrates the other. Finding ways to hold these conversations decreases the later occurrence of more serious problems and enhances collaboration (Friend & Cook, 2007).

Maintenance of Confidentiality

Teachers know that information about students must be kept confidential, and the same is true for co-teachers. However, they may have to be particularly careful on this matter because of their shared work. They may discuss students as they walk down the hall together or eat lunch at school or stand in line at a local fast food restaurant. Their concern and commitment is admirable—but inadvertently violating confidentiality through their conversations must be avoided. A second type of confidentiality also must be considered: Co-teachers should avoid discussing the co-taught class unless both teachers are present. This simple strategy can eliminate miscommunication and misunderstanding.

Acknowledgment of Pet Peeves

All teachers have pet peeves. These may relate to students (for example, pen-tapping, tilting a chair back, addressing a teacher by saying "Hey" instead of using the teacher's name), teachers (for example, borrowing pens or pencils, getting materials or supplies out and not putting them back), or any aspect of teaching and learning (for example, duplicated materials that are not clear, dirty computer keyboards). Co-teachers are advised to touch base with each other about their pet peeves. Discussing them, even if the items that concern one teacher are very different from those of the other, ensures that miscommunication is avoided. For example, if one teacher does not want students to go to lockers for any reason after the bell rings, the other teacher (who is not as adamant on this point) can follow the partner's wishes.

Other Topics Concerning Partnership

_____
_____
_____
_____
_____

Topics for Classroom and Behavior Management

In addition to exploring topics related to partnership, co-teachers should spend a few moments clarifying their expectations regarding classroom and behavior management. One way of thinking about these matters is to consider each professional: Especially as teachers gain experience, they usually develop automaticity related to how they operate a classroom and respond to student behaviors. That is, they don't even need to think about the ways they expect students to enter the class, complete assignments, or work with their classmates. However, when two teachers share a classroom, they may find that each person's automaticity is interrupted and conversations about managing the classroom and students' behavior become vital to creating a new set of procedures acceptable to both educators. Here are examples of topics in this category:

Use of Space for Instruction

Many of the co-teaching approaches include simultaneous instruction of multiple groups of students. For the students in the groups to be able to focus their attention, complete their own work, and avoid disrupting others' work, teachers need to analyze their physical space and identify ways to use it for maximum effectiveness. They might decide that a low bookcase now against a wall would serve as an effective sight and sound barrier if placed at a right angle to the wall. They could decide, since their classroom has whiteboards on two opposing walls, that parallel teaching can best be managed by having half the students face one board while the other half faces the opposite direction. The goal is to think about space use and take into account the potential for noise and distraction when two teachers work together.

Tolerance for Noise and Strategies for Keeping Noise at an Acceptable Level

Co-teachers may wish to discuss each person's tolerance of the noise of a classroom in which several activities are occurring simultaneously. Many of the most effective co-taught classrooms would sound noisy to a guest, but the noise is purposeful. To manage noise, both teachers should instruct students to speak in low voices, and they also have to remind themselves and each other to do the same. Teachers also should discuss where each person should stand or sit during instruction. For example, in parallel teaching, teachers might want to sit during instruction if they face each other across the room. Otherwise their voices may carry to the other side. If noise seems to bother a student, the teachers may want to find a desk carrel for the student or provide a single desk tucked into a quiet corner of the classroom for that student to use. If either teacher is bothered by the classroom noise level, the topic should be added to the agenda for the next shared planning session so that options to resolve this dilemma can be discussed.

Organizational Routines

This topic concerns all the details of classroom operation. What do students do with assignments as they are completed? What are acceptable activities for them to do if they complete work before the end of the lesson? Do students need to ask permission to go to the restroom or simply pick up a hall pass and leave? How do students line up to leave the classroom? May students pack up before the bell rings? You can probably list at least another dozen procedures that are part of day-to-day classroom life. Special educators who are in any single classroom for only a short time generally follow the procedures established by the general education teacher—they just need to be aware of what those procedures are. If co-teachers are together all day or even half of each day (a pattern in some elementary schools), then more negotiation on classroom procedures might be in order. Also, if some students with disabilities cannot follow typical class procedures—as could happen for a student with autism, for example—the special educator should make recommendations for addressing the student's needs.

Procedures for Substitute Teachers

Co-teachers sometimes discuss what will happen in the class when a substitute teacher is necessary. As with many of the topics mentioned in this chapter, no single answer is recommended for integrating substitute teachers into co-teaching. Some teachers will ask a substitute teacher to assume a helping role because the remaining partner knows the instruction that comes next and can manage the class. If a co-teacher will be absent for an extended time, a decision about the responsibilities of the substitute teacher may depend on that person's experience in the classroom and skills related to the subject area or the special education.

Safety Procedures

Co-teachers should discuss general safety procedures, including those related to evacuating the school in case of fire, taking shelter in case of tornadoes or earthquakes, or responding to any other type of school emergency. Both teachers should know where to go and how to access any supplies kept in the classroom. In addition, co-teachers should be sure that both know whether any students need special consideration in case of an emergency. For example, the fire alarm may badly frighten a student who wears hearing aids. Similarly, the teachers should know what procedure to follow in case of a fire (when elevators are not accessible) for a student whose class is on the second floor.

Classroom Rules

Co-teachers should check that they agree on the rules established for the shared classroom. If schoolwide positive behavior supports are in place, the expectations set for classrooms should be acceptable. However, if your school leaves the matter of rules to each teacher, this can be an important topic. One teacher may post rules and consequences that are mostly negative (for example, do not leave your seat unless given permission; first consequence is moving your name from the green circle to the yellow and the second consequence is moving to red and losing minutes of recess). The other teacher may strongly prefer a system based on positive consequences (for example, treat your materials and those of others with respect; each student earns "cash" for appropriate behavior that is used once every two weeks to purchase privileges or tangible rewards). A discussion may help to address this topic as well as a related one—that is, the extent to which rules are enforced consistently.

Discipline Procedures for Specific Students

Even if all organizational procedures are clarified and classroom discipline addressed, some students with disabilities will need further accommodations. A student with ADHD may need a standing desk (similar to a lectern) so that he can move as he works. A student with a learning disability may need a contract through which she earns rewards for each 10 minutes of on-task behavior. General education teachers may not be aware of the requirement of these kinds of individualized behavior supports, and special educators should ensure that they are provided as outlined by the IEP or determined to be necessary as an informal form of support for the student.

Other Topics Concerning Classroom and Behavior Management

_____

_____

_____

_____

Instructional Practices in the Co-Taught Classroom

An extensive array of professional literature exists on effectively teaching diverse groups of students in general education classrooms (Acrey, Johnstone, & Milligan, 2005; Friend & Bursuck, 2009; Tomlinson, 2001; vanGarderen & Whittaker, 2006). There are not enough pages in this handbook for a thorough discussion of this topic, but a few points can be made about instruction and a few examples provided of co-teachers making maximum use of two teachers to enhance teaching and learning.

A question that co-teachers should spend considerable time addressing is this: How is the instruction in the co-taught classroom different than it would be in a classroom with one teacher? The companion question that speaks to students with disabilities is this: How are the goals on the IEP (and, depending on state policy and student characteristics, the objectives) being incorporated into the instruction occurring in the co-taught class? Both questions illustrate the purpose of co-teaching. First, it should result in instruction that is more intense, more varied, and more creative than the teaching that one person could do. Second, the positive variations in instruction establish a basis for differentiating instruction so that supports and specialized instruction for students with disabilities can be offered in a seamless and non-stigmatizing way.

You may know that the vocabulary related to instruction for students with disabilities has several components (Friend & Bursuck, 2009). First, IDEA notes that the team writing the IEP must designate the supplementary aids and services (SAS) that are to be provided to students with disabilities so they can receive their education in general education settings. The law also stipulates that students should receive accommodations and modifications. Accommodations are the tools that assist students to learn the curriculum and include extended time for tests, audiotaped textbooks, use of calculators or manipulatives, and so on. Modifications are reductions in the curricular competencies such as having a student learn about fractions but not how to add them. Finally, the term *differentiation*, not part of IDEA, is used to capture the innumerable tools and strategies teachers proactively use to ensure that all students—regardless of their unique needs—learn the curriculum (Heacox, 2002; Tomlinson, 2001). Some professionals refer to differentiated instruction as responsive teaching.

Many models—some simple and some complex—for differentiating instruction can be found in the professional literature. The following model is based on the essential elements of the teaching/learning process, and each is illustrated with a few examples that are especially appropriate for a co-taught class.

Learning Environment

Environment refers to the physical as well as the social and emotional climate of the classroom. Co-teachers can consider whether items dangling from the ceiling are distracting to students with attention problems as might be the bouncing computer screen savers usually in view. Environment also can include lighting (do any students need lighting that is brighter or dimmer than other students?), the arrangement of classroom furniture (do any students need an individual desk even though other students are seated across from each other at tables?), and student seating (does a student who uses a wheelchair need to be placed in the center of the class instead of the more convenient corner because the former location enhances interactions with peers?). Environment related to classroom climate may include whether soft music is played during some activities, whether students burst excitedly into the classroom in the morning or enter with whispers, and whether students may study sitting in a comfortable chair instead of a traditional chair at a desk. If you scan the classroom and think about classroom procedures, you will identify many other items that contribute to the environment.

Curriculum Content

Nearly all students with disabilities are expected to achieve proficiency in the same curriculum as their nondisabled peers, and this is a reasonable expectation for most. However, some students may benefit from slight changes to curriculum that take into account their needs. For example, some students may master effect written at a lower reading level than those for other students. Some students may learn about idioms as required in the middle school curriculum, but they draw pictures to illustrate their understanding instead of writing stories that use idioms. Co-teachers should remember that their instruction for students with disabilities should be designed to address curriculum competencies or standards, but there often are many ways that concepts can be introduced, practiced, and learning demonstrated.

Ways that Teachers Deliver Instruction

Teaching procedures suited to specific student characteristics can enhance learning. For example, some students will follow directions far more accurately if teachers state each one clearly and succinctly, briefly write each part of the directions on the board, and have students repeat directions back after they are given. At the same time, this procedure does not interfere with any student's learning, even if it is not essential for them. Similarly, many students benefit from extensive use of visuals that clarify the instruction. Students in warm climates may not understand what snow really is and so may fail to understand the subtleties of a story about polar bears. Students learning about an agricultural culture may not be able to comprehend its character because they live in a large city and have never been outside of it. Co-teachers should provide vicarious experiences for students when they lack personal experiences related to the content being taught.

One other aspect of teaching should be mentioned. For students who struggle with learning, connecting the instruction from the day before, previewing the instruction for the current day, and summarizing instruction as it concludes can facilitate learning. Again, this type of procedure harms no student but illustrates appropriate differentiation.

Opportunities for Students to Learn Concepts and Skills

How students engage in learning could be the most important aspect of effective co-teaching instruction. For example, a middle school class read a play about freedom of speech. Students were given many options for demonstrating their learning. One teacher worked with students as they prepared posters that would advertise the play if it was released as a major motion picture. The other teacher assisted students as they wrote a different ending to the play. A third group of students worked on a webquest related to first amendment rights. In another classroom, the teachers engaged students by increasing their participation throughout instruction. They asked students to repeat answers aloud, used individual whiteboards so that all students could write (and erase) responses, and had students vote for the answers they believed were correct. All these strategies and the many others that teachers devise are designed to involve students visually, auditorily, tactilely, and kinesthetically.

Strategies for Evaluating Student Learning

Grading student work in co-taught classes sometimes is a matter of great debate, and no single solution to the grading dilemma exists. What is most important is that the approach to grading is fair but at the same time considers students' special needs (Silva, Munk, & Bursuck, 2005). For example, some teachers count students' in-class work and homework more than tests because the students are diligent but do not perform well on tests. Other teachers do just the opposite, minimizing the grades for homework for students who do well on tests but who seldom complete homework. Yet other teachers create options for students to earn extra credit to make up for missed assignments and poor test scores. As with many other parts of instruction, co-teachers should discuss what strategies fit the entire class and which are only available to students with disabilities by virtue of their status as protected by special education law.

Ways that the Adults Work Together

Co-teachers cycle back to discussions about the difference between their two-teacher classroom and a one-teacher classroom in this conversation. However, they also should consider how any other available adults are integrated into classroom instruction. In kindergarten, parent volunteers may enable co-teachers to create additional small groups for station teaching. In elementary school, responsibilities for paraprofessionals may be the topic for discussion. In middle and high schools, student teachers or interns could be the additional adults who can contribute to instruction. Set in the context of differentiation, co-teachers should consider how these adults can help to increase instructional intensity and individualization, keep discipline problems to a minimum, and improve student engagement—while at the same time recognizing that volunteers, paraprofessionals, and student interns should not assume teacher responsibilities.

Other Topics Concerning Instruction

_____
_____
_____
_____

As you can see from the various topics covered in this chapter, many of the small classroom matters you may take for granted when you teach alone may be become a focus for attention when you co-teach. The conversations that co-teachers have in order to analyze their preferences, expectations, and assumptions about teaching and learning are central to creating solid programs that quickly develop into strong partnerships producing improved outcomes for students.

For Further Thought

1. Of the topics related to co-teachers' partnerships, which do you find the most important? What topics would you add to the list? How does your list compare to the list prepared by your teaching partner?

2. When you think about classroom management, what are your priorities? How do your priorities compare with those of your co-teacher? What changes could be made to the classroom management practices you already have in place to take into account both professionals' perspectives?

3. If a visitor came to your co-taught class, what evidence would she see of instruction that has been tailored to meet the needs of students with disabilities? How do the changes made relate to students' IEPs?

Taking Action

1. Consider using professional development opportunities at your school to refine professionals' collaboration skills. Through book study, speakers, video, or other means, learn more about how to raise and discuss difficult or awkward matters, ask questions and make statements in ways that enhance communication, be aware of nonverbal communication, respond to resistance, and negotiate. Skills for collaboration will enhance co-teaching partnerships, a specialized application of collaboration.

2. Ask the special educators at your school to present a brief presentation on behavior difficulties related to students with disabilities. For example, they could outline the relationship between language delays and aggressive behavior or the unique behavioral needs of students with autism spectrum disorders. Use this information as the basis for discussing behavior strategies that should be promoted throughout the school.

3. Share ideas with colleagues for differentiating in the co-taught classroom. The goal should be for each professional to learn at least three new ways to better meet student needs.

References

Acrey, C., Johnstone, C., & Milligan, C. (2005). Using universal design to unlock the potential for academic achievement of at-risk learners. *Teaching Exceptional Children, 38*(2), 22-31.

Abell, M. M., Bauder, D. K., & Simmons T. J. (2005). Access to the general curriculum: A curriculum and instruction perspective for educators. *Intervention in School and Clinic, 41*, 82-86.

Dieker, L.A. (2001). What are the characteristics of "effective" middle and high school co-taught teams for students with disabilities? *Preventing School Failure, 46*(1), 14-23.

Friend, M., & Bursuck, W. D. (2009). *Including students with special needs: A practical guide for classroom teachers* (5th edition). Boston: Allyn and Bacon.

Friend, M., & Cook, L. (2007). *Interactions: Collaboration skills for school professionals* (5th edition). Boston: Allyn and Bacon.

Gately, S. E., & Gately, F. J. (2001). Understanding co-teaching components. *Teaching Exceptional Children, 33*(4), 40-47.

Heacox, D. (2002). *Differentiating instruction in the regular classroom: How to reach and teach all all learners, grades 3-12*. Minneapolis, MN: Free Spirit Publishing.

Hourcade, J., & Bauwens, J. (2002). *Cooperative teaching: Re-building and sharing the schoolhouse* (4th edition). Austin, TX: Pro-Ed.

Lawrence-Brown, D. (2004). Differentiated instruction: Inclusive strategies for standards-based learning that benefit the whole class. *American Secondary Education, 32*(3). 34-62.

Lewis, S. G., & Batts, K. (2005). How to implement differentiated instruction? Adjust, adjust, adjust. *Journal of Staff Development, 26*(4), 26-31.

Murray, C. (2004). Clarifying collaborative roles in urban high schools: General educators' perspectives. *Teaching Exceptional Children, 36*(5), 44-51.

Silva, M., Munk, D. D., & Bursuck, W. D. (2005). Grading adaptations for students with disabilities. *Intervention in School and Clinic, 41*, 87-98.

Tomlinson, C. A. (2001). *How to differentiate instruction in mixed-ability classrooms.* Alexandria, VA: Association for Supervision and Curriculum Development.

vanGarderen, D., & Whittaker, C. (2006). Planning differentiated, multicultural instruction for secondary inclusive classrooms. *Teaching Exceptional Children, 38*(3), 12-20.

Wasburn-Moses, L. (2005). Roles and responsibilities of secondary special education teachers in an age of reform. *Remedial and Special Education, 26*, 151-158.

Chapter 4 Appendix

• • • • • •

The first item in this appendix is an adaptation of the Colorado Assessment of Co-Teaching (CO-ACT), a research-based instrument drawing from the essential components of co-teaching outlined in Chapter 1. It considers co-teachers' working relationships, the use of two professionals in the classroom, and the structure and preparation for the co-teaching program. The remaining pages provide a checklist for assessing parity in the classroom, a tool for exploring how co-teachers can significantly enhance instructional options over those possible when just one teacher is in the classroom, and several websites that offer a wealth of information on effective instructional practices for students with disabilities and other special needs.

Colorado Assessment of Co-Teaching (CO-ACT)

This instrument has been adapted from the Colorado Assessment of Co-teaching (CO-ACT) (Adams, Cessna, & Friend, 1993). The items included in this assessment are associated with effective co-teaching teams. If you are new to co-teaching, responding to this questionnaire will help you prepare for your new role and responsibilities. If you are a veteran co-teacher, you may use this to reflect on and refine your skills. Co-teaching partners may find it especially helpful to discuss their responses.

Factor I: Personal Prerequisites. Personal prerequisites are the skills and characteristics that each teacher brings to a co-teaching situation. They include your attitudes and beliefs, experience, teaching style, interpersonal skills, and knowledge specific to your discipline or subject.

Factor II: The Professional Relationship. The Professional relationship describes the collaborative interaction of the co-teachers. It includes the sense of parity between co-teachers, the willingness to learn from one another, the ability to communicate and work toward a shared goal and the extent to which key decisions and accountability for those decisions are shared.

Factor III: Classroom Dynamics. Classroom dynamics are the actions that give added benefit to the co-taught classroom. These include your perceptions of how teaching and learning occur, your knowledge of the academic and social curriculum, and the range of individualizing strategies you use.

For each of the following, respond in two ways. Rate the **importance** of each statement by checking responses on the scale to the left. Also, rate the **extent to which the item is present in your co-teaching situation** by checking responses on the scale to the right.

How much do you agree that each factor is *important* in co-teaching?

IMPORTANCE

How much do you agree that each factor *describes your co-teaching situation?*

PRESENCE

IMPORTANCE					Personal Prerequisites	PRESENCE				
strongly disagree	disagree	neutral	agree	strongly agree		strongly disagree	disagree	neutral	agree	strongly agree
1	2	3	4	5	1. Co-teachers are confident in their skills as individual teachers.	1	2	3	4	5
1	2	3	4	5	2. The special educator has skills to suggest instructional strategies to meet unique student needs.	1	2	3	4	5
1	2	3	4	5	3. The general education teacher acknowledges the need for accommodations for individual students in the co-taught classroom.	1	2	3	4	5
1	2	3	4	5	4. The general education teacher has strong knowledge of the curriculum content.	1	2	3	4	5
1	2	3	4	5	5. The special educator is confident in his/her knowledge of the curriculum content.	1	2	3	4	5
1	2	3	4	5	6. Co-teachers are willing to share their knowledge and skills with each other.	1	2	3	4	5
1	2	3	4	5	7. Co-teachers have effective communication skills.	1	2	3	4	5
1	2	3	4	5	8. Co-teachers have strong classroom management skills.	1	2	3	4	5
1	2	3	4	5	9. Co-teachers are eager to expand their skills.	1	2	3	4	5
1	2	3	4	5	10. Co-teachers believe co-teaching is worth the effort.	1	2	3	4	5

The Professional Relationship

IMPORTANCE					The Professional Relationship	PRESENCE				
strongly disagree	disagree	neutral	agree	strongly agree		strongly disagree	disagree	neutral	agree	strongly agree
1	2	3	4	5	11. Co-teachers are committed to building and maintaining their professional relationship.	1	2	3	4	5
1	2	3	4	5	12. Co-teachers share a philosophy about learning and teaching.	1	2	3	4	5
1	2	3	4	5	13. Co-teachers respect each other's professionalism.	1	2	3	4	5
1	2	3	4	5	14. Co-teachers share common goals for the co-taught classroom.	1	2	3	4	5
1	2	3	4	5	15. Each co-teacher has a distinct but essential purpose in the co-taught class.	1	2	3	4	5
1	2	3	4	5	16. Co-teachers acknowledge their areas of weakness and seek assistance.	1	2	3	4	5
1	2	3	4	5	17. Co-teachers are able to release control to their co-teacher.	1	2	3	4	5
1	2	3	4	5	18. Co-teachers share equal responsibility for what happens in the classroom.	1	2	3	4	5
1	2	3	4	5	19. Co-teachers regularly set time aside for joint planning.	1	2	3	4	5
1	2	3	4	5	20. Co-teachers make important decisions together.	1	2	3	4	5
1	2	3	4	5	21. Co-teachers carry their part of the workload.	1	2	3	4	5
1	2	3	4	5	22. During a lesson co-teachers can sense the others' thoughts and direction.	1	2	3	4	5
1	2	3	4	5	23. Co-teachers share the gentle and the tough roles.	1	2	3	4	5
1	2	3	4	5	24. Classroom space is shared so that both teachers have a work space.	1	2	3	4	5
1	2	3	4	5	25. Co-teachers jointly assess what's working and what isn't on a regular basis.	1	2	3	4	5
1	2	3	4	5	26. Co-teachers communicate during lessons to facilitate student learning.	1	2	3	4	5
1	2	3	4	5	27. Co-teachers use collaborative strategies for problem solving.	1	2	3	4	5

PRESENCE

IMPORTANCE

Importance: strongly disagree	disagree	neutral	agree	strongly agree	Classroom Dynamics	Presence: strongly disagree	disagree	neutral	agree	strongly agree
1	2	3	4	5	28. Both teachers are responsible for teaching all students in the co-taught classroom.	1	2	3	4	5
1	2	3	4	5	29. Students with disabilities are intermingled with students without disabilities.	1	2	3	4	5
1	2	3	4	5	30. Students receive individual help and structure to complete assignments.	1	2	3	4	5
1	2	3	4	5	31. Co-teachers use a variety of student grouping arrangements.	1	2	3	4	5
1	2	3	4	5	32. Co-teachers use a variety of co-teaching structures/formats.	1	2	3	4	5
1	2	3	4	5	33. Students with disabilities are provided with accommodations.	1	2	3	4	5
1	2	3	4	5	34. Instructional delivery in co-taught classes involves the presentation of information in a variety of ways.	1	2	3	4	5
1	2	3	4	5	35. Co-teachers make continual adjustments to ensure student success.	1	2	3	4	5
1	2	3	4	5	36. Co-teachers employ a variety of methods to assess students' progress.	1	2	3	4	5
1	2	3	4	5	37. Co-teachers monitor students' academic progress on a regular basis.	1	2	3	4	5
1	2	3	4	5	38. Co-teachers adapt assessment tools and procedures as needed.	1	2	3	4	5
1	2	3	4	5	39. Instructional delivery in co-taught classes is different from what occurs in other classes taught by the general education teacher.	1	2	3	4	5

SCORING INSTRUCTIONS

Add the scores you gave each item in each factor for all of the items.
Write the total for each factor in the appropriate blank.

	Importance	Presence
Factor I	_____	Factor I _____
Factor II	_____	Factor II _____
Factor III	_____	Factor III _____
Total	_____	**Total** _____

Add down the columns to determine the instrument total.

UNDERSTANDING YOUR SCORES

This section contains a description of each of the factors and information on the average scores obtained by exemplary co-teaching teams. It is intended to help you understand your responses.

Factor I: Personal Prerequisites. Personal prerequisites are the skills and characteristics that each teacher brings to a co-teaching situation. They include your teaching style, knowledge specific to your discipline or subject, and your contribution to the classroom. The average total score of exemplary co-teaching teams on this factor is: Importance - 66.1   Presence - 68.03

Factor II: The Professional Relationship. The professional relationship describes the collaborative interaction of the co-teachers. It includes the sense of parity between co-teachers, the ability to work toward a shared goal and the extent to which key decisions are shared, and accountability for those decisions. The average total score of exemplary co-teaching teams on this factor is: Importance - 37.28   Presence - 38.69

Factor III: Classroom Dynamics. Classroom dynamics are the beliefs and actions that give added benefit to the co-taught classroom. These include your perceptions of how teaching and learning occur, your knowledge of the academic and social curriculum, and the range of individualizing strategies you use. The average total score of exemplary co-teaching teams on this factor is: Importance - 60.88 Presence - 62.75

Total score. One additional way of considering your responses on the instrument is to look at your total score. When you consider this score, it is important to keep in mind that co-teaching has many variations. A high overall score typically reflects co-teaching that relies extensively on a collaborative relationship and might be referred to as collaborative co-teaching. While teachers report that collaborative co-teaching is very fulfilling for them and very beneficial for students, because of circumstances it may not be the most preferred or feasible type for you. Other less intensive approaches to co-teaching can also be effective. The average total score of exemplary co-teaching teams on this factor is: Importance - 163.92 Presence - 169.08

Parity, Parity, Parity

How do you and your co-teaching partner convey to students that your teaching relationship is truly collaborative, that it is a partnership based on parity? The following checklist might help you to think through ideas about how you, your teaching partner, and students can observe parity or its absence! NOTE: Do keep in mind that which of the following parity signals pertain to your situation depends on many factors.

Already Do	Should Do	Not Applicable	
_____	_____	_____	1. Both teachers' names are on the board or posted in the classroom.
_____	_____	_____	2. Both teachers' names are on schedules and report cards.
_____	_____	_____	3. Both teachers' handwriting is on student assignments (that is, each teacher participates in grading).
_____	_____	_____	4. Both teachers have space for personal belongings.
_____	_____	_____	5. Both teachers have similar furniture (i.e. desks, chairs).
_____	_____	_____	6. Both teachers take a lead role in the classroom.
_____	_____	_____	7. Teacher talk during instruction is approximately equal.
_____	_____	_____	8. Both teachers give directions orpermission without checking with the other teacher.
_____	_____	_____	9. Both teachers work with all students.
_____	_____	_____	10. Both teachers are considered teachers by the students.

Making an Instructional Difference in Co-Teaching

One advantage that co-teachers have over other teachers is that they can provide greater differentiation in the classroom, addressing a wider diversity of student needs with maximum effectiveness. With your co-teacher, discuss how each of the dimensions of differentiating may look in a one-teacher versus a two-teacher classroom. Emphasize how to increase instructional intensity through the active involvement of both teachers.

Dimension of Differentiation	One-Teacher Classroom	Two-Teacher Classroom
Content and Materials		
Classroom Physical and Social Environment		
Instructional Strategies		
Student Learning Strategies		
Evaluation of Student Learning		
Collaboration		

Internet Resources on Effective Instruction

- *National Center to Improve Practice in Special Education Through Technology, Media, and Materials*
  http://www2.edc.org/ncip
  Offers suggestions on using research-based teaching practices with students with disabilities and other special needs.

- *Success for All Foundation*
  http://www.successforall.com
  Program information for elementary, middle and secondary levels. Links to published research about Success for All programs.

- *Teaching Every Student* (TES)
  http://www.cast.org/teachingeverystudent/
  One of the original websites addressing information on universal design for learning. A free book on the topic can be downloaded from this website.

- *Classroom Connect*
  http://corporate.classroom.com
  Ideas to simplify teachers' jobs, including a variety of classroom management and other teaching tips.

- *ProQuest K-12*
  http://www.homeworkcentral.com
  Extensive links to online libraries of lesson plans that include modifications for students with special needs, a homework help area, and state curriculum guides.

- *Teachers Helping Teachers*
  http://www.pacificnet.net/~mandel/
  Practical ideas about specific teaching problems from actual teachers in the field, lesson plans, teachers' forums, and curriculum materials.

- *Study Guides and Strategies*
  http://www.studygs.net
  Provides study guides as well as strategies for preparing for and taking tests. The site provides study skills resources including several links to study skills guides and interactive tutorials. Materials are available in 25 different languages.

- *Council of Chief State School Officers* (CCSSO)
  http://www.ccsso.org
  Testing and grading policies being used around the country.

- *Teach-nology*
  http://www.teach-nology.com/tutorials/teaching/differentiate/planning/
  Offers step-by-step instructions for planning differentiation in general education classrooms.

- *Flemington-Raritan Regional School District* (Flemington, NJ)
  http://www.frsd.k12.nj.us/rfmslibrarylab/di/differentiated_instruction.htm
  Contains a great list of websites that offer detailed information on accommodating students with special needs in planning, delivery, and assessment of instruction.

- The *Leon County (FL) Schools*
  http://www.tandl.leon.k12.fl.us/lang/DIindex.html
  Fosters differentiated instruction at all grade levels; includes links to additional reading material and sample lesson plans that incorporate the principles of differentiating.

- *InterventionCentral.org*
  http://www.interventioncentral.org/htmdocs/interventions/cbmwarehouse.php
  Many instructional materials for graphing scores, adjusting readabilities, implementing reading fluency/math computation probes, collecting CBM/CBA data, etc.   In the section where you can adjust readabilities for individual readers, the computer automatically counts words per a page and per a row so that it saves teachers' time to prepare for lessons or tests.

- *Pomperaug Regional School District* (CT)
  http://www.region15.org/curriculum/graphicorg.html
  Extensive collection of graphic organizers available in English and Spanish (pdf and Word formats provided for each).

- *abcteach*
  http://www.abcteach.com/
  Practical instructional materials such as writing prompts, graphic organizers, research formats, and portfolio forms for pre-K through high school. Clip art for developing original instructional materials, flashcards, options for designing an original crossword, shape book, word wall, word unscramble, word search, math worksheets, and sudoku by using abctools. Everything is free!

- *Florida's Instructional Technology Resource Center* (ITRC)
  http://www.itrc.ucf.edu
  Ways to improve your teaching and thus improve student outcomes through technology

- *The Center for Applied Special Technology*
  http://www.cast.org
  Helpful suggestions for the universal design of learning materials and teaching practices to reduce the need for developing special accommodations and modifications for individual students in general education classes.

- *The Center for Effective Collaboration and Practice*
  http://cecp.air.org
  Federally funded organization designed to promote effective educational practices for students with emotional and behavior problems.

- *Behavior Advisor*
  http://www.behavioradvisor.com/
  Award-winning website that includes thousands of ideas and links for addressing student behavior problems, whether they are simple or complex. This is a site that is best visited when there is time to browse.

- *RTI Wire*
  http://www.jimwrightonline.com/php/rti/rti_wire.php
  With the move to identify students needing assistance based on their response to intervention, this website is invaluable. It includes an explanation of RTI, tools for designing interventions, data collection templates, and more.

Chapter 5
The Logistics of Creating and Sustaining Co-Teaching Programs

• • • • • •

That which we persist in doing becomes easier, not that the task itself has become easier, but that our ability to perform it has improved.

-Ralph Waldo Emerson

Chapter Objectives

1. Identify an appropriate amount of planning time to seek for preparing to co-teach, and list ideas for using planning time effectively.

2. Describe appropriate class size and composition for a co-taught class or section.

3. Outline strategies for addressing issues related to developing a school schedule that includes co-teaching.

4. Explore considerations in determining staffing for co-teaching programs.

Many co-teachers find they can work out their classroom partnerships and develop strategies for addressing the diverse needs of the students they teach. They learn to experiment with co-

• • • • •

teaching approaches, blending them and using variations of them to make the classroom a focused, motivating, and learning-rich setting for their pupils. They are confident in their own skills for instructing their pupils and assisting them to reach their potential.

However, they often express frustration about several issues related to co-teaching logistics. These include finding adequate shared planning time, ensuring that the number and needs of the students who comprise their classes is appropriate, and scheduling co-teaching when many other competing priorities and complexities exist. These are the topics for this chapter.

Shared Planning Time

By far the most common dilemma expressed among teachers and administrators setting up co-teaching programs is the difficulty of arranging common planning time for co-teaching partners (Dieker & Murawski, 2003; Hobbs & Rose, 2000; Spencer, 2005). Certainly, co-teachers must have some time to discuss their instruction and the students for whom they are responsible. However, sometimes the expectations for this shared planning time just are not realistic.

When I ask educators how much planning time they think would be sufficient, they often give responses like these:

- One planning period each day for each co-taught class.
- One planning period each week with each teacher with whom I co-teach.
- At least two hours per week, split among the co-teaching partners.

If funding and staffing levels support this amount of planning time, of course it is a wonderful situation. However, in most schools these options are not realistic. For example, a special educator who co-teaches with three or four other teachers would, in the first example of the time requested, barely have time to teach. Even in the second example, a special educator co-teaching with four colleagues would spend nearly an entire instructional day per week just on planning for co-teaching. Neither of these scenarios is likely to occur.

In many cases, a different way of thinking about planning time is more likely to lead to constructive solutions. Specifically, professionals could look for what is called *macro-planning* time and then supplement it with some *planning on the fly*. This combination permits collaboration in exactly the way it should occur: Teachers share key decisions, but divide much of the labor of planning. They then can confer to be sure they are prepared for the planned instruction.

Macro-Planning Time

Rather than daily or weekly planning time, professionals can try to find periodic, high quality planning time at which they sketch instructional plans for periods of two, three, or even four weeks. The goal of such planning time is to ensure that both educators know what curriculum is upcoming and identify ways it can be delivered so that all students are successful. Here are ways that teachers and administrators are successfully creating this type of planning time.

Early planning during the summer. Especially for new co-teachers, getting a head start on the school year by planning during the summer can be very effective. Co-teachers might seek funding for two or three half-days of planning time during which they address many of the start-up issues that are mentioned throughout this book and also focus on instructional planning. Their goals should be to map out in detail the first three or four weeks of the school year and to outline the topics and co-teaching approaches for at least the first month.

Compensated after-school planning. Once the school year begins, some professionals find the simplest solution for planning is to schedule it outside school hours—but to receive some type of compensation for this extra effort. Two options seem reasonable: (a) pay for off-contract work and (b) professional development credit accumulated across a school year. In the first option, co-teachers agree to meet for two hours per month on their own time—before or after school or on weekends. They may complete a simple form of some type to demonstrate accountability, and they receive pay for this time at their hourly rate. The payment will not make much difference in teachers' overall income, but it is an acknowledgement that co-teachers have planning responsibilities that go beyond those of other teachers. The second option, professional development credit, is similar, but it enables co-teachers to receive credit for their planning. If a district requires that teachers acquire, say, 15 clock hours of professional development time to receive one credit, co-teachers could, over a semester or year, log their planning outside school hours on an accountability form documenting the time spent meeting and receive this credit. In districts striving to increase co-teaching, after–school planning sessions for credit are advertised to all personnel so that teachers can meet at an arranged location to share ideas as they plan. Sometimes the location for these sessions is changed from month to month to make it convenient for everyone.

Alternative use of professional time. Many school districts have several teacher professional development days scheduled across the school year. In some districts, co-teachers may opt to be exempt from any planned activity for a certain amount of time (say, two hours) each time one of these days is on the calendar. The teachers use this time for planning. This option has the advantages of occurring during the day and eliminating the need for additional resources. However, depending on the topic of the staff development, missing part of it might be problematic.

Use of substitute teachers. Before the current era of school reform and accountability, placing substitute teachers in classrooms to free co-teachers for planning was relatively common. Now, though, this option has many drawbacks in addition to the practical ones— finding skilled substitute teachers and the funding to pay them. Because of increasing achievement standards, many administrators are reluctant to permit teachers to miss instructional time in order to plan for co-teaching. In addition, teachers released for planning through substitute teachers must plan appropriate instructional activities for their students and then ensure, after the planning, that those activities were completed. Many teachers find it just is not worth the time required to use this option.

If substitute teachers seem viable to you, some suggestions can streamline this type of planning option. First, the co-teachers should agree they will share the sub. That is, one month the sub will cover for the general education teacher and the special education teacher will use already-assigned planning time to meet. The next month, the sub will cover for the special education teacher and the general education teacher will use assigned planning time.

In this way, neither professional is required to miss too much time with students. Second, it sometimes is helpful to arrange for this option at the beginning of the school year with a substitute teacher known as a pro. That is, if the substitute knows in August that a particularly date in September, October, November, and so on will be scheduled for this type of subbing, the person can reserve those dates for the school. At the same time, teachers then have a predictable schedule for macro-planning and can work out among themselves and with their administrator how best to use the substitute teacher's time.

Collaboration among staff members. Finding common planning time can become much easier if everyone works together. For example, in some schools, principals and assistant principals agree to cover a class period each week or specific number of minutes for a co-teaching partnership needing planning time. One teacher uses assigned planning time and the other is released by the administrator. Other personnel—counselors, school psychologists, and literacy coaches, for example—also could contribute small amounts of time to facilitate co-teaching planning. Principals and other school professionals who do not have assigned class groups certainly have busy schedules and many responsibilities, but this approach can foster a collaborative school culture, can permit those professionals to spend meaningful time in classrooms, and can help co-teachers to feel truly supported.

Other ways to collaborate for macro-planning time also can be worked out. For example, in some high schools teachers receive compensation for extra duties they complete, usually during their planning period. Thus, a teacher may be paid to release co-teachers so they can plan. In other schools, co-teachers are exempt from a duty (for example, hall duty, bus duty, study hall) so that they can find time to plan with their partner. In yet other schools, when more than one special education teacher is employed, the teachers may take turns covering classes for a general education teacher in order to create shared planning time (Dieker, 2007). That is, once every four weeks Special Educator A covers for the general education teacher co-teaching with Special Educator B. Likewise, Special

Educator B covers once each month for the general education teacher working with Special Educator A. No one misses a significant amount of instructional time, but a common planning time is created.

Other shared planning time options. Creative administrators and other professionals have found many other strategies to arrange common planning time for co-teachers.

- Some elementary school principals are able to arrange for all the teachers in a grade level to have related arts (that is, art, music, physical education, library, technology) at one time. The special educator is also freed at this time so the grade level can plan and co-teachers can confer.

- In a few districts, the school calendar includes periodic days (as often as once per week, as seldom as once per grading period) designated for students' late arrival or early dismissal. In these schools, the standard school day is lengthened a bit, and then on the shortened days, students come late or leave early so professionals have additional time for professional development, conferences, and other essential activities. Co-teaching planning sometimes occurs during such times.

- Some co-teachers take advantage of electronic communication. They use e-mail or text messaging to discuss classroom issues, brainstorm ideas for upcoming lessons, and discuss differentiation strategies.

Use of Macro-Planning Time

Regardless of how macro-planning time is arranged, the secret to success is using it wisely (Hawbaker, Balong, Buckwalter, & Runyon, 2001). Think about what happens when you finally—after working with students all day—have a chance to interact with a colleague. Often a period of "venting and chatting" occurs. Teachers share their recollections about what occurred at last weekend's football game, or they discuss the details of the movies they recently saw, or they trade stories about their students' most recent accomplishments or challenges. Co-teachers must learn that any macro-planning meeting should have an agenda so that the precious shared time is spent on key topics. A sample agenda that could be laminated, written on with a water-based marker, and re-used for the entire year, is included in the appendix at the end of this chapter. Alternatively, a copy of the agenda could be made for each planning meeting. Another idea for creating an agenda is to keep a notebook or clipboard where both teachers can easily access it. Each professional adds items to the agenda as they are identified, and this shared agenda is the basis for the next planning meeting.

In most instances, general education teachers should come to the planning meeting already having thought about the upcoming instruction—the chapters to be covered, themes to be addressed, projects that must be completed, and so on. After briefly sharing the information with the special educator, the partners should discuss how the material could best be taught and learned with co-teaching, the division of the material, and the selection of co-teaching approaches. Teachers then should turn their attention to the expectations for students, including questions such as these: What accommodations might be needed because of students' varying reading levels? Which students might need manipulatives or calculators? Which assignments are so long and complex that they should be divided into smaller segments for some students?

Unless a student is having a crisis or a situation demands that a student be the primary topic of conversation, it is recommended that specific conversations about students be reserved until the last part of the meeting. The careful planning that goes on benefits all students, and the risk is that, if students are discussed first, the curricular and instructional parts of planning are short-changed since teachers sometimes become very engaged in discussing particular student issues. If specific conversations about students are focused on data related to areas for improvement, they usually can be completed quickly and constructively. Planning usually ends with a brief discussion of instruction that already has occurred and reflection on its effectiveness.

After the meeting, the special educator takes responsibility for completing any significant adaptations or modifications needed for class materials or activities. For example, if middle school students need an audiotaped study guide to support their learning the chapter on World War II, the special educator prepares it. Similarly, if worksheets or activity packets should have highlighting to assist student learning, this is a task the special educator usually would complete.

Does this approach to macro-planning make sense to you? It is equitable—both teachers have separate as well as shared responsibilities. It also is efficient—the limited time available for planning is used for maximum advantage. The process is summarized in Figure 5.1.

Keep in mind that the specifics are not as important as the principles on which this planning model is based: that good quality, periodic planning often can lead to successful co-teaching, that meetings should be business-like and centered around an agenda, and that tackling instructional issues goes a long way toward meeting individual student needs but those unique needs have a place in planning, too.

Planning on the Fly

If co-teachers create a schedule of macro-planning meetings and ensure that both know the key concepts about to be addressed, the instructional dilemmas that students may encounter, and the expectations for projects and activities, co-teachers then can fill in the details with planning on the fly. That is, they can quickly touch base about day-to-day teaching matters using brief snippets of time such as these:

Warm-ups. In many classrooms, instruction begins with some type of warm-up activity. Co-teachers can use this time for planning on the fly. At the start of the class period, or in elementary schools when the special educator arrives for co-teaching, the students are directed to complete, independently or possibly with a partner, an appropriate instructional activity. The activity may be a problem similar to the type introduced the day before, it might be a question students are to answer by using their textbooks, or it might be a reading assignment. Students are directed to do the activity without interrupting the teachers unless an emergency arises. The three or four minutes for the activity create an opportunity for the co-teachers to touch base to be sure they're ready for the day's lesson.

Review and predict. For elementary students or in secondary classrooms when the special educator comes in for the second half of a block-scheduled class (a topic addressed later in this chapter),

Figure 5.1
The Co-Teaching Planning Process

BEFORE THE MEETING

General education teacher gathers key information about upcoming curriculum, projects and activities, and other core content and brings this material to the meeting.

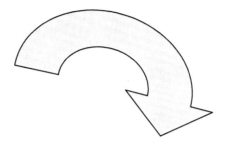

DURING THE MEETING

General and special education teachers decide which co-teaching approaches to use, how to group students, which aspects of the instruction may pose difficulties, and which projects may be overwhelming for students. Individual student matters are also discussed. The meeting concludes with review and reflection on past instruction.

AFTER THE MEETING

Special education teacher prepares the unique differentiated materials and strategies necessary for the instruction, plan for meeting IEP goals within the curriculum, and prepares to incorporate learning process into the content.

planning on the fly can be part of the instruction itself. When the special educator enters the room, one of the two teachers asks students to briefly review what they have been doing and learning. This helps the special educator get oriented to the day's classroom activities. One of the teachers then asks the students to relate the activity that is to occur with both teachers present. Clearly this option implies that the general education teacher has prepared students in advance for co-teaching, but that often will happen just because of scheduling. However, having students stop to review their learning and think about what they've been told will occur next is sound instructional practice and, like warm-ups, helps the special educator prepare for the lesson.

Passing period prepping. Although certainly not ideal, if middle and high school co-teachers have used macro-planning so they both have a sketch of upcoming instruction, quite a bit of last-minute planning can occur during the minutes between class periods, provided the special educator can get to the classroom before the bell rings. For example, the general education teacher might explain that he would like to continue discussing the similarities between two periods in history while the special education teacher takes small groups of students to the side to fill in the sections of the class timeline on which they have been working. This option leaves more of the day-to-day details to the general educator, but it still permits brief conversations that, based on the more detailed macro-planning, can foster effective teaching and learning.

Instructional videos. If teachers need a bit of extra time to discuss their plans and an appropriate instructional video is available, showing the video can give the teachers 10 or 15 minutes of time to plan. Although the quality of this time is not high because of the need to monitor students, it can occasionally help the teachers find the valuable minutes that will make the teaching and learning more successful.

Although every teacher would like more planning time and a few school districts are able to provide planning time for co-teachers every day, the strategies above can provide enough time to make co-teaching feasible and deliberate.

Class Composition and Size

A second significant logistics issue for co-teaching programs relates to students. In this section, the most common dilemmas regarding students are addressed, including which students with disabilities are appropriate candidates for co-teaching, what the overall co-taught class size should be, how many students with disabilities should be in a co-taught class, and who the other students should be.

Students with Disabilities Who Benefit from Co-Teaching

If a simple formula could be used to decide whether any particular student with disabilities would benefit from co-teaching, assigning students would become a routine part of scheduling. Unfortunately, no such formula exists. Even the easy—and obvious—answer that the student's IEP team makes this decision does not provide the guidance that most educators are looking for.

The starting point to begin a discussion about which students with disabilities to place in a co-taught class is with the purpose of the co-teaching program. Is the primary intent to ensure that students achieve success on high stakes tests? Is it to provide access to the general curriculum for all students? Is it to implement an inclusive service delivery option in order to meet the requirement that all core academic content be taught by highly qualified teachers? The answers to questions such as these will influence decisions about which students should be assigned to co-taught classes. No single correct answer can be given, but two examples might help you to see how to think about this critical matter.

In the first case, co-teaching is implemented in an elementary school so that an inclusive education can be offered even to students with fairly significant needs. Because co-teaching is an all-day arrangement (as exists in some parts of New York and elsewhere around the country) or a half-day arrangement in which a co-teacher and a paraprofessional each spend half a day in a classroom and then swap places for the other half of the day, the students assigned to the co-taught class generally have intellectual disabilities, significant learning disabilities, or serious behavior problems. This arrangement is, in essence, offering fulltime special education services to the students in the classes, and so the presumption would be that only students with significant needs should be enrolled in the classes. Students with more mild needs are likely to be placed in other classrooms in which consultation or a small amount of co-teaching is available, or a period of pullout services occurs as often as needed as determined by the IEP team.

In the second case, the basis for the middle school or high school co-teaching program is to address students' need to access core academic content from teachers trained in that subject matter. Thus, students with documented disabilities in math are assigned to the co-taught eighth grade Algebra I class so they learn from the math teacher while their individual needs are assessed, addressed, and monitored by the special educator. Students whose IEPs address only English are not assigned to this co-taught section.

In an ideal world, all students with disabilities would participate in general education classes, and every class could be co-taught. In the reality of today, professionals must think through the nature and intensity of student needs and the type of support necessary to fulfill the requirements of IDEA. For some students, co-teaching is the answer. For others, the support of a paraprofessional is adequate. For yet others, some combination of co-taught, paraprofessional-supported, and limited pullout service is warranted. And for just a few students, a more restrictive setting (for example, receiving all core academic instruction in a special education setting) is the only choice, most often because of behavior needs and occasionally because of learning needs.

Ultimately, the most common dilemma in schools that implement co-teaching programs is over-serving students. That is, students who in a traditional program received 45 minutes or one class period of instruction in a pullout special education program suddenly are seen to need the support of co-teaching in all academic classes. This is a serious issue administrators and teachers should be alert for and avoid. Even though the argument that reading levels present a barrier to learning across subjects, particularly in secondary settings, is understandable, the use of technology and other strategies of differentiation must be explored. Inadvertently creating an expectation that every student with a disability in a general education setting must have co-teaching leads to frustration and the belief that co-teaching requires additional staffing.

Class Size

Some co-teachers proudly explain that not only are there two teachers in the class for which they are responsible, they also arranged for their section to have far fewer students than comparable sections, perhaps 18 students when other elementary classes have 24, or perhaps 20 students when other sections of ninth-grade English have 25 or 28 students. If resources permit this approach, it would be hard to argue that it is not better for instruction. However, in most situations, resources are stretched to accomplish these smaller class sizes, and they may not be warranted.

Remember that the core element of co-teaching is having two professionals who are both actively engaged in the teaching and learning process. When class size is also reduced, it is a form of "double-dipping." That is, there are two teachers who also get a preferential class size. This topic is a matter for discussion with administrators.

However, the opposite can happen, too. In some schools, especially high schools, all students are distributed among the sections of a course such as biology so that each is populated at about 25 students. Then, after the fact, a group of five or six students with disabilities is placed into one section. Now the enrollment of that section is 31 students, larger than any of the other sections. This approach sets co-teachers up to encounter problems that are inevitable when a class is overcrowded and some of the students already have significant learning or behavior needs. It also undermines a school culture of inclusiveness.

Number of Students with Disabilities in a Co-Taught Class

A few school districts set guidelines for the number of students with disabilities who should be in a co-taught class. Policies related to this matter generally arise from legal issues and their resolution or from negotiations with local professional teachers' associations. If you are not affected by either of those factors, you might find these guidelines helpful.

The quick answer to this issue is this: There should be enough students with disabilities in a class so that providing services is feasible across the school but not so many that it becomes impossible to keep the instructional pace necessary for student success. The precise number that statement translates to can vary, but generally at the elementary level, no more than 25 percent of a class should be made up of students with disabilities, and preferably, the percentage would be slightly lower. At the secondary level, as many as 33 percent of the students in a class might have disabilities, but when the number goes beyond that level, maintaining the quality and pacing of instruction often becomes impossible. Of course, the number of students who have significant behavior problems would affect the actual number as would the type of disabilities they have and the intensity of supports they need.

Other factors also must be taken into account. Teachers sometimes ask whether a student should be "counted" in the percentages even if the student does not have a disability in that content area—the answer is usually not. However, this type of question is a signal of the need for a school to go back to the topic of inclusiveness since it indicates educators are concerned about who they are being asked to teach.

The Other Students in Co-Taught Classes

In many cases, the key issue is not the number of students with disabilities in the co-taught class. Instead, it is the characteristics of the rest of the students assigned to the class. At least two issues seem to affect this broader matter of class composition: (a) understandings of the individuals who assign students to class; and (b) a school's decisions about levels of classes or tracking.

Assigning students to classes. Many middle and high school co-teachers lament that they hear this logic from counselors or other schedulers as an explanation for why their classes are overloaded with students at risk: "But there are two of you in there!" This logic is seriously flawed. The only students entitled to be assigned to a co-taught class are the students with IEPs for whom this constitutes their special education. If other students, by the luck of the draw, wind up in the class, that is wonderful for them. However, when many at-risk students are placed in the class, it often becomes impossible for the teachers to maintain the necessary instructional pace. In addition, grouping many students with learning problems in one class often leads to a multiplication of behavior problems.

The related issue on scheduling students is assigning *all* students with IEPs to particular classes or sections. As noted earlier in this chapter, some students with IEPs do not need the intensity of co-teaching to accomplish their educational goals, and some students need it only for certain classes. Professionals should stay aware that placing all students with disabilities in co-taught classes becomes a "one size fits all" approach, the antithesis of what special education is supposed to be.

The tricky topic of tracking. If you are a middle school or high school co-teacher and your class of 26 includes 14 students with IEPs, five students who are considered at risk for learning failure, three students who are English language learners, two students who are often absent or truant, and two students who just happened to be assigned to that section, the chance of having a significant positive impact on student achievement is limited. If this type of pattern is common in your school, it is unlikely co-teaching can be sustainable; keeping up the necessary pace for the curriculum becomes nearly impossible. You might try discussing this matter with the person responsible for scheduling since sometimes classes are composed without realizing the problems caused. Alternatively, this is a conversation to have with your principal. What this type of arrangement suggests is that a school is tracking students.

Although it is not possible in this book to adequately explore the topic of heterogeneous versus homogeneous grouping for instruction, a few comments might help prompt conversation with your colleagues. First, generally speaking, data on grouping suggest that heterogeneous grouping is preferred for elementary and middle school (Burris, & Welner, 2005; Burris, Heubert, & Levin, 2006; Ford, 2005; Lotan, 2006). High achievers are not penalized by this approach, and students who struggle have access to positive models and peer learning. In late middle school and high school, natural groupings occur as the curriculum becomes differentiated by courses. For example, in many middle schools, only students who are ready for Algebra I take it in eighth grade, thus creating a high achievers group. This pattern continues in high school as students take advanced placement, international baccalaureate, or dual enrollment courses.

The dilemma occurs when several levels of courses are established and then the assumption evolves that students with disabilities should be in low-track classes. Most students with disabilities do not have intellectual disabilities (a topic addressed in more detail in Chapter 2), and assigning them to classes with a slower curriculum or one that is less rigorous often is inappropriate. At one large middle school committed to three levels of all core classes, the principal recently decided that co-teaching should occur in the middle level of classes so that students with disabilities can be encouraged to truly reach their potential. This type of thinking merits attention at all schools.

Finally, one comment must be added related to elementary schools. Although still not common, some elementary schools are beginning to do their own version of tracking when multiple sections exist. Even if not done for the entire day, reading/language arts and math may be tracked. Research supports skill grouping in order to address the development of reading skills (for example, Kuhn, 2004), but elementary educators should keep in mind that the goal of today's education is to have students, even struggling readers, access the curriculum. If they do not participate in activities with their peers, this goal is unlikely to be realized.

Scheduling and Co-Teaching

The matter of scheduling is one that each school implementing co-teaching struggles to address. That is partly because there is no simple formula that applies across schools. Instead, there are some procedures that can guide scheduling and some general principles for making scheduling feasible.

Procedures for Scheduling Co-Teaching

When professionals tackle scheduling in a proactive manner, these are the general steps they follow:

1. Identify students to be served and their needs. The first step in scheduling co-teaching is to know student needs. With

IEPs on the table, teachers should carefully review each student's assessed needs, the resulting IEP goals (and, for some, objectives), and the type of service that will lead to achieving goals. In new programs this may eventually necessitate revising some IEPs.

2. Recent high stakes test data should be directly considered in determining student needs.

3. Once the list of students, with test data and service needs, is compiled by grade level, team, or special educator caseload, the number of sections of co-taught classes, resource or support classes, and separate core content classes can be calculated.

4. Next, the specific classes or section for co-teaching can be identified as can the teachers to be assigned to them. Also, the times for resource and separate core instruction can be determined. In elementary schools, if more than one special educator is available, students should be divided by grade level, but caseloads should be kept equitable. In middle schools, it is preferable for special educators to be assigned by teams. In junior high schools, special educators may work within one or possibly two subject areas. In high schools using interdisciplinary 9th grade teams, a middle school model is appropriate (that is, the special educator assigned to a team). In traditional high schools, special educators usually should work by department. Of course, in small schools where there is just one special educator, decisions about co-teaching should be prioritized based either on (a) the number of students in grade levels or sections, or (b) subjects areas considered most essential for student success (for example, English I or algebra).

In the appendix that follows this chapter, you can find a form that facilitates this process of basing co-teaching on student needs. Of course, in small schools when only one section of a class exists at a grade level, scheduling is not an issue. In large schools, this process may have to be tweaked because of the number of students. In middle schools, the number of students on a team has to be monitored to be sure the number does not get too high.

General Principles for Scheduling

In addition to following procedures such as those outlined above, here are a few additional suggestions about scheduling to facilitate co-teaching:

- Co-teaching seldom should be the only special education service available in an inclusive school. Consultation, resource/study skills/strategies classes, and separate core instructional classes also are likely to be needed, particularly in large schools.

- In small schools (and even some large ones), scheduling students by hand instead of using a computer program is the only way to resolve scheduling problems.

- Although not always true, scheduling students with disabilities first rather than last generally results in fewer scheduling problems. For example, stating that a student with a disability cannot take a course in a high school because it was filled with typical learners before the student ever had a chance to enroll is a violation of the student's civil rights.

- When using software to schedule students, the best strategy is to create concurrent sections of a course, one section that populates with students who are typical learners (or who do not have an IEP goal in that subject area) and one that populates only students with disabilities. By capping each section (for example, at 22 for the first section and 6 for the second) and then blending the two sections once scheduling is completed, most of the assignments of students can be accomplished within the larger scheduling procedure. Then the few problems that arise can be addressed with manual scheduling.

- In mature co-teaching programs, special educators often co-teach in three, four, or even five classes each day. In new programs, one or two locations may be more appropriate. When special educators must provide support to students in six, seven, or even more classes, some of the service should be designated as consultation on the IEP since meaningful co-teaching in that number of classes clearly is not possible.

- Some co-teaching might occur for less than an entire class period and less than daily. Particularly in middle and high school block classes, co-teaching may only be able to be offered for half a block, or co-teaching may be divided across the span of two weeks across two sections, based on what is occurring in each class (for example, three days in one class and then two in the other with the reverse the next week). Professionals usually are less than satisfied with this type of service, but it should at least be considered when examining student needs and services to which students are entitled.

- To prioritize co-teaching, different factors should be considered. In elementary schools, it may be the number of students in a grade level needing service (for example, can co-teaching be justified for two kindergartners with mild needs in one classroom?) In middle schools, it may be students' performance and needs in core academic subjects. In high schools, it might be based on high stakes testing necessary to earn a standard diploma.

Number of Teachers Needed for Co-Teaching

Teachers and administrators often indicate that co-teaching is not feasible without an allocation of special education teacher time beyond what typically is provided in a traditional special education program (Russ, Chiang, Rylance, & Bongers, 2001). Sometimes this may be true, especially when special educators are the case managers for 30 or more students. However, if caseloads are 25 or fewer students, then the conversation should focus on how much co-teaching should occur, in which subject areas, and how existing staff members can be used most effectively. The first two topics have already been addressed in earlier sections; the latter is briefly considered here. Although you should check on local policies regarding some of the ideas that follow, these suggestions— combined with those already presented in the section on scheduling—might help you and your colleagues find ways to make co-teaching seem feasible. Remember that these ideas might also be mixed and matched to address your specific needs.

- Staffing sometimes is an issue because special educators are accustomed to working only with the students on their caseloads. Blending might help. For example, in an elementary school, if two special educators stagger their schedules so that pullout services can be available for nearly the entire day, then students needing more intensive support can receive it while co-teaching is still a feasible service delivery option (but not all day for all students). However, both teachers—not just one—may serve some students. In high school, teachers should divide co-teaching by subject area, not students. That is, one special educator co-teaches in English (all levels) while another co-teaches in math (all levels). Each will assist in serving the other's students, but co-teaching will be far more likely to occur meaningfully.

- Another alternative is for paraprofessional support to be provided in some classes. For example, in a middle school keyboarding class, a paraprofessional might offer support to students because a co-teacher is not needed. The same might be true for high school vocational or related arts classes.

- Duplication of services should be examined. If an appropriate self-contained class is offering a subject needed by just a few students with disabilities who are not members of the class, perhaps they should attend that class for instruction instead of creating a second section of it. This option usually exists in elementary and middle schools. When separate sections are needed, special educators and administrators should consider blending two grade levels or two similar subjects to avoid having time periods or sections with just three or four students.

- Ensure that special educators' time is devoted to meeting the needs of students with IEPs. In some schools, the implementing of early intervening services (EIS) and response-to-intervention (RtI) for students at-risk is adding to the responsibilities of special educators. That is, instead of these initiatives being implemented by general education teachers or math or reading specialists, they are assigned to the special education teachers. If new special educator time is allocated, that is fine. However, when special educators already have caseloads that approach the maximum allowed (or caseloads that are typical by local practice), if an hour or more of their time is assigned to teach remedial reading or other subjects to at-risk learners, the services that must be offered to the students with disabilities assigned to them cannot be met. This matter sometimes becomes a legal issue as well as an ethical one.

- Consider other types of support for some situations. In elementary schools, parent volunteers can provide support in classrooms. This clearly is not a special education service, but if the need is for an extra set of hands then perhaps special education support is not required. In middle schools located close to the high school or a college, future teacher organizations or student interns might serve a similar role. In high schools, a service learning course can be created for students who have completed required coursework. Students enrolling in the course can work as teaching assistants in courses they have previously taken, serving as tutors to some students and generally helping the teacher with the diversity of learners. Other forms of peer tutoring also can provide support when co-teaching might not be necessary (McMaster, Fuchs, & Fuchs, 2006).

The point of these ideas is to prompt you to think carefully about creative solutions to staffing contemporary programs for students with disabilities. That often means thinking beyond the traditional configurations in which services have been provided and drawing on all support services in a school. Of course, the types of services and amount provided must be accurately reflected on students' IEPs.

For Further Thought

1. What are your own expectations for planning time for co-teaching? Are they realistic? How could macro-planning time help to address them?

2. Think about special educators' responsibilities for providing support to students with disabilities as well as students at risk for failure. How do you think they should balance these responsibilities?

3. What might be the opportunities and drawbacks of scheduling some co-teaching less than daily? What factors would you consider most important in making a decision regarding this aspect of scheduling?

4. In Chapter 1 you learned about key concepts, including collaboration and inclusiveness. What do these concepts suggest related to staffing for co-teaching programs? What issues related to teachers' sense of control and beliefs about the way co-teaching should be set up affect their beliefs about staffing?

Taking Action

1. With your grade level, team, department, or colleague work group, identify three strategies for creating planning time that might be feasible. Propose them to your administrator with a rationale for why they could work and how they would enhance co-teaching in your school.

2. Review the composition of each current or proposed co-taught class in your school. How many of the students in each are typical learners? Students with disabilities? Students with other special needs? What adjustments are needed for next semester or next year? How will you propose this issue be addressed? Create a plan with your administrator so that class composition improves.

3. With your administrator, review the schedule for co-teaching and identify key concerns. Discuss ideas from the chapter that could help to address these scheduling concerns. You might include a larger, all-staff discussion of the implications of creating sections of classes that have too many students with significant learning and behavior needs.

References

Burris, C. C., & Welner, K. G. (2005). A special section on the achievement gap—Closing the achievement gap by detracking. *Phi Delta Kappan, 86*, 594.

Burris, C. C., Heubert, J. P., & Levin, H. M. (2006). Accelerating mathematics achievement using heterogeneous grouping. *American Educational Research Journal, 43*, 105-136.

Dieker, L. (2007). *Demystifying secondary inclusion: Powerful schoolwide & classroom strategies.* Port Chester, NY: Dude Publishing.

Dieker, L. A., & Murawski, W. W. (2003). Co-teaching at the secondary level: Unique issues, current trends, and suggestions for success. *High School Journal, 86*(4), 1-13.

Ford, M. P. (2005). *Differentiation through flexible grouping: Successfully reaching all readers.* Naperville, IL: Learning Point Associates/North Central Regional Educational Laboratory (NCREL). (ERIC Document Reproduction Service No. ED489510)

Hawbaker, B. W., Balong, M., Buckwalter, S., & Runyon, S. (2001). Building a strong BASE of support for all students through coplanning. *Teaching Exceptional Children, 33*(4), 24-30.

Hobbs, S. F., & Rose, E. (2000). Dealing with reality. In M. S. E. Fishbaugh (Ed.), *The collaboration guide for early career educators* (pp. 185-200). Baltimore: Paul H. Brookes.

Kuhn, M. (2004). Helping students become accurate, expressive readers: Fluency instruction for small groups. *Reading Teacher, 58*, 338-344.

Lotan, R. (2006). Teaching teachers to build equitable classrooms. *Theory into Practice*, 45(1), 32-39.

McMaster, K. L., Fuchs, D., & Fuchs, L. S. (2006). Research on peer-assisted learning strategies: The promise and limitations of peer-mediated instruction. *Reading & Writing Quarterly, 22*(1), 5-25.

Russ, S., Chiang, B., Rylance, B. J., & Bongers, J. (2001). Caseload in special education: An integration of research findings. *Exceptional Children, 67*, 161-172.

Spencer, S. A. (2005). Lynne Cook and June Downing: The practicalities of collaboration in special education service delivery. *Intervention in School and Clinic, 40*, 296-300.

Chapter 5 Appendix:
Planning for and Scheduling Co-Teaching

• • • • • •

The worksheets in this appendix are designed to assist you in identifying and resolving some of the logistical barriers to co-teaching. They are intended to help school professionals think "outside the box" in order to make co-teaching a realistic service option.

Sample Planning Agenda

Date _____ Teachers/subject _____

Upcoming curriculum topics/units/lessons (8 minutes)

Co-teaching arrangements and assignments (17 minutes)

Challenges and strategies to help students succeed (15 minutes)

Individual student matters (15 minutes)

Housekeeping/Logistics (5 minutes)

Co-Teaching Based on Student Needs

This form or an adaptation of it can be used to map out student needs and the types of services which will ensure students achieve their goals. Once completed for each student, professionals can use the information to decide on the amount of co-teaching needed or number of co-taught sections needed as well as the need for other services and instructional settings.

Name	Eligibility[1]	Test Data	Service by Subject						Notes
			English/ LA	Math	Science	Social Studies	Related Arts	Other	

[1]Eligibility: Use district eligibility categories (for example, LD, ED, MR, OHI)

Service by subject:

CON=Consultation   CT= Co-teaching
RES=Resource/support   SCI=Separate core instruction
Other A= _____   Other B= _____

Questions to Guide the Scheduling Process

The exact procedure followed to create an effective and feasible co-teaching schedule depends completely on individual school characteristics, student needs, and staffing patterns, and so no simple formula can be offered. Here is a sample of questions that may help professionals think about important variables that affect scheduling.

All School Levels

- How many students with disabilities attend the school? At what grade levels?
- Based on students' assessed needs, what type of service (if any) should each student receive (see chart on page 150)?
- How many classes/sections of each service are needed? Which grade levels or which courses?
  - o Co-teaching
  - o Resource/support (non-core instruction)
  - o Separate core instruction (in academic areas)
  - o Self-contained

- Which students should receive consultation or other indirect services instead of or in addition to other services?
- Which grades or courses are priorities for co-teaching? (These grades or courses should be staffed first.)
- What are the priorities for separate core instruction? (These sections should be scheduled next.)

Elementary Schools

- By grade level, how could students across sections be grouped for services (for example, moving students class to class for skill instruction in reading or math)?
- How could all support personnel be deployed to support student learning needs without duplicating services (for example, the speech-language therapist, reading specialist, paraprofessionals—who could go where)?
- How can special educators be assigned so that caseloads are equitable and services are not duplicated (for example, one special educator might serve kindergarten, first grade, and fourth grade and provide some service to a student with significant disabilities who comes to one of those classes)?

Middle Schools

- If more than one grade-level team exists, could all students with disabilities be placed on a single team? How could those students be distributed across sections on that team so that the class composition is heterogeneous?
- How could separate sections be created to cross, if necessary, teams and grade levels (for example, a separate section of math for the few 6th and 7th grade students who must have this intense instruction)?
- Could any students needing separate instruction receive it in an existing (and appropriate) self-contained class (for example, a student with LD receiving English instruction in a class for students with emotional disabilities)?
- If classes are leveled, how could students with disabilities be scheduled into middle level (not low level) classes so that achievement can more easily be fostered and class heterogeneity maintained?

High Schools

- Which courses prepare students for high stakes tests? These should be the priority for co-teaching.
- Are other factors priorities? Examples include beginning with 9th and 10th grade classes, focusing on English and algebra, and so on.
- If the high school is arranged in small school learning communities, how can necessary separate resource or separate instruction be scheduled as a priority in order to cross those learning communities?
- How should special educators be assigned to co-teaching? In traditional high schools, assignments may be by department/subject area, while in schools arranged in small schools or with interdisciplinary teams, assignments may be by community or team.

Chapter 6
Co-Teaching Program Development and Evaluation

● ● ● ● ● ●

Anyone who has never made a mistake
has never tried anything new.

-Albert Einstein

Chapter Objectives

1. Develop a plan for creating and sustaining co-teaching as a service delivery option for students with disabilities.

2. Discuss each step in a program development process, including the purpose for each and dilemmas that may occur.

3. Outline a rationale and procedures for evaluating co-teaching programs.

4. Use data about co-teaching to improve programs and report their status to colleagues, parents, and others.

Across the country, the implementation of co-teaching and the extent to which it has been integrated into special education and overall school services vary tremendously. Some co-teaching partners feel like they are completely on their own, that they received permission to co-teach but no school-level expectation has been set and no plan exists to expand the service model. Some school leaders have made a strong commitment to co-teaching and other inclusive practices, and all the professionals in the school are aware of them and frequently participate either directly or indirectly. These schools may routinely provide co-teaching to students with disabilities, even if it is not common across other schools in the district. In some districts, co-teaching is integral to inclusive practices, and it is clearly a mandated part of the service delivery continuum. Finally, a few states have set specific guidelines based on the *No Child Left Behind Act* (NCLB) and the *Individuals with Disabilities Education Improvement Act* (IDEA) that relate to providing special education services through co-teaching. In those states, many school districts are designing and implementing co-teaching programs.

Which situation are you in? If it is the first one, this chapter may function mostly as a vision of what might eventually be possible. If it is any of the other situations, this chapter may serve as a roadmap for developing a strong co-teaching program that quickly becomes central to services for students with disabilities and other special needs. If your co-teaching program is struggling, the information presented in the following sections may provide insight into ways to analyze the problems and find ways to resolve them. And if your co-teaching program is mature, this chapter can offer strategies for renewing the commitment and ensuring that it is sustainable.

Development of a Co-Teaching Program

Many models for program development have been offered in the professional literature (for example, Hord, Rutherford, Huling-Austin, & Hall, 1987; Schlechty, 2006), and much of this work is based on how to create school change, regardless of the particular program or service under discussion (Schwahn & Spady, 1998). The stages outlined in the following sections represent the process generally recommended.

Stage 1: Establish the Program and Its Goals

Approaching the task of developing a co-teaching program with a clean slate can be the simplest of situations: No history of past practices exists and the deliberate and carefully-planned implementation can pay off with quick results for students and teachers. Here are the topics addressed in beginning to plan for a new program:

Clarify intent.

It may seem obvious, but the first conversations about co-teaching should focus on purpose: Why are we doing this? What will co-teaching look like once it has been fully implemented? Who will be directly or indirectly affected by co-teaching? Quick answers to these questions are not enough, especially to the first one. Co-teaching may be undertaken to address student achievement, the matter of highly qualified teachers, or curriculum access, or other reasons. Through the planning, implementation, evaluation, and sustaining phases, the reason for the program should always be the focus. It is the "true north" for the program. To clarify intent, visits to existing programs and conversations with others who have implemented co-teaching sometimes are helpful.

Establish a planning structure.

The next early step in planning is to create the appropriate structure for moving the concept to reality. Usually, this involves identifying a team of individuals who will complete detailed preparation work and, possibly, serve as the first implementers. Identifying a diverse team is important. It should include strong advocates of co-teaching, at least one professional who is opposed to or uncertain about it, an administrator, and possibly a parent, related services provider, and paraprofessional (depending on program intent and situational factors). Of course, this team will need to meet on a regular basis, and so the logistics of holding meetings must be arranged.

Assess needs and set goals.

Even before detailed planning occurs, the team should take into account the needs to be addressed. They might prepare a brief survey to distribute to teachers regarding the instructional dilemmas for students with disabilities found in existing programs, or query staff members on the importance of a coordinated system of services that include students with disabilities, but also those who receive speech/language services only, ESL or bilingual services, or others. Parents of students with disabilities could be asked to complete a brief questionnaire distributed at annual review meetings. This needs assessment activity provides the planning team with information on the perspectives of the various audiences for a program, but it also alerts everyone that changes are going to occur. If a mismatch is found between the perceived needs and the original intent of the program, discussions should occur to resolve the discrepancy. Also, team members should remember that needs assessment provides understanding of *perceived* needs. Other needs may exist (often identified by administrators or others with broad perspective) even if not reported by those participating in the needs assessment activity.

Stage 2: Plan for Implementation

Once a team is formed, an overall structure is created for the program development process, initial information is gathered, and more detailed planning can occur. It includes these activities:

Identify and describe the ideal outcome.

Team members should clarify at this point specific goals for the program (Friend & Pope, 2005). Is co-teaching intended to reduce the number of students served in self-contained classes by 25 percent over the next five years? Ensure that all students with disabilities taking high stakes tests have core academic instruction delivered by a teacher who is not just highly qualified but also fully licensed? Improve the achievement scores for students with learning and behavior disabilities by at least 5 percent per year over the next five years? There is not a single right set of goals; the key is to ensure goals are specific enough that participants and others will know when they are met or if difficulties are being encountered in achieving them. Team members should keep in mind that the goals for a co-teaching program should address any legal issues related to services for students with disabilities.

Specify component parts.

With specific goals in mind attention can turn to determining what component parts have to be in place for co-teaching to be initiated. Is co-teaching to occur in just language arts in the elementary school? In all core academic areas in the middle school? Only in 9th grade in the high school? How much planning time should be provided for initial participants? What about professional development needs? As a team moves through this very detailed planning, they are likely to need an extended period of time to meet, and if a retreat can be arranged that often is ideal.

Match the context and resources.

To this point, nothing has been said about being realistic. It's not that attending to reality is not important; it's that attending to it too soon narrows thinking and limits program options. However, as implementation draws near, the planning team should discuss the balance between what would be ideal and what can occur now. The team may need to prioritize elements of the plan that has been made if not all aspects of it can be implemented immediately. In addition, the team should stop at this point to ensure that co-teaching is being integrated with other initiatives so that it does not seem like an unrelated, added-on program. This point helps school professionals from feeling like co-teaching is a burden added to their already-hectic professional lives.

Design implementation strategies.

The conversation about matching context and resources to the co-teaching program goals creates the basis for final decisions about the scope of initial implementation. These decisions are the ones that represent the essence of what the new program will be on the first day it is implemented. Decision-making at this point also should narrow the priorities for staff development: Do implementers need more co-teaching training? Do they need further reading on working with students with disabilities in general education settings? Do they need additional clarification of goals? Is a priority topic to expand understanding of differentiated instruction?

Establish timelines.

In some schools the timeline is dictated by the need to meet federal or state requirements. If this is the case, you may not have much input into it. However, in many schools implementation timelines are a decision made by the planning team. The advice on this matter is to start small so that any problems that arise likewise will be small and addressed more easily than if they are school wide. Beginning co-teaching with certain students, in certain grades or courses, or only a specified number of participants is realistic. For subsequent years, the planned timeline can include ensuring the program is solid and then expanding it to other areas or students.

Stage 3: Prepare for Implementation

With planning accomplished, the next stage is making all necessary preparations for implementation. This is a point at which a diverse team can be particularly skillful. Members are likely to think of different aspects of the planned program that need attention, and their collective efforts will lead to a careful completion of the final part of planning.

Create awareness.

All potential implementers of co-teaching should receive a brief explanation of the goals for the program, the role expectations, the support they will receive, and an opportunity to discuss co-teaching and ask questions concerning it. At this pre-implementation point, teachers' concerns are likely to be personal. General education teachers may wonder which students with disabilities they would be expected to teach and how those students' achievement scores would affect their personnel evaluations. They might express reluctance at the thought of another teacher in the classroom, including concern about being evaluated by the teaching partners. Special education teachers may be overwhelmed by the amount of content they would have to learn and the anticipated pacing. They may note that they can best reach their students in a small, structured, special education setting. Comments such as these need to be aired and addressed.

Select implementers.

The overview of co-teaching just described should be followed by a request for volunteers. Although mature co-teaching programs should be part of all school services and not a matter just for volunteers, initial implementers should be enthusiastic rather than reluctant, and so only those who are eager to participate should be selected. However, principals have an obligation at this point to continue discussing inclusive practices and co-teaching, building the expectation that eventually any teacher in the school could be asked to participate.

Make logistical arrangements.

While the first co-teachers are being identified, many other activities should occur. Teachers should indicate preference for teaching partners, but principals should make the final decisions. Professional development far more detailed than the awareness training should be arranged for the co-teachers, and planning time should be scheduled. The composition of co-taught classes should be carefully monitored and specific students scheduled into the two-teacher classes. If any specific materials are needed in the co-taught class, those should be purchased. Materials most likely requested are related to differentiated instruction—from smartboards to individual whiteboards, from a folding screen to divide the classroom to a table the teachers can share as a desk. In addition, the selected co-teachers and administrators should develop a specific strategy for gathering data related to the impact of the program on student learning and behavior.

Prepare personnel.

Once all the detailed preparations are completed, all staff members in the school should learn a little more about co-teaching. Principals may devote a segment of time to the topic at the opening of the school year, or they may add information about the program to a faculty meeting agenda. The teachers implementing should have periodic opportunities to continue their learning about co-teaching and to discuss their early implementation.

Design an evaluation.

Strategies for evaluation should be considered as programs are being developed. The fundamental question is this: How will you know whether co-teaching has accomplished the intended goals? The topic of evaluation is addressed more thoroughly later in this chapter.

Stage 4: Implement the Co-Teaching Program

If you're sensing that most of the work of establishing co-teaching services occurs during the planning phase, you are correct. If care has been taken to thoroughly discuss issues, to address logistics, and to select appropriate participants, implementation should be relatively straightforward. That is not to say, though, that problems won't occur (Dieker, 2007; Villa, Thousand, & Nevin, 2004). One very common characteristic of co-teaching is that, because so many factors converge to make it successful, one or more unanticipated changes can cause problems. Perhaps the principal is transferred over the summer to another school, or one of the teachers decides to move to another city. Because of an error in scheduling, one class may have too many students with disabilities and class re-assignments must be made. Expecting a start-up without challenges is not realistic. It is how those challenges are faced that can determine the success of the first year of a program. The following are activities for early implementation:

Expand professional development activities.

Throughout the first year of implementation, co-teachers should continue with professional development. They might undertake a book study on differentiated instruction or attend a conference to learn more about inclusive practices. They might participate in staff development offered by their district or enroll in a university course. Alternatively, as discussed in Chapter 5, they might receive continuing education credits for planning they do. During the first year, bits of information should continue to be shared with all staff members, too. For example, in one school teachers had many questions about two students with autism who had enrolled. The co-teachers working with one of the students prepared a brief presentation on how they helped him succeed in the general education classroom. Of course, information sessions should include opportunities for teachers to ask questions about the new co-teaching program.

Carry out program activities.

Despite any last-minutes changes due to unforeseen situations, co-teachers should carry out the program, deliberately experimenting with the co-teaching approaches, discussing what works and what does not, and gradually building a strong professional relationship that benefits students. Keep in mind that the learning curve during the first year can be steep, and so co-teachers should make sure that they talk about their shared work frequently and seek assistance if either of them senses that the marriage is struggling.

Evaluate the program.

Even as implementation begins, the plan for evaluating the effectiveness of co-teaching should be in place. Data should be gathered even during the first quarter of the school year so that adjustments can be made if problems are noted. This topic is considered in more detail later in this chapter.

Stage 5: Maintain the Co-Teaching Program

Chances are that your co-teaching program is part of larger efforts related to inclusive practices (Waldron & McLeskey, 2001). That makes it especially important that the planning team has looked beyond getting the program started to keeping it viable as an option for educating students with disabilities.

Refine the program.

Based on data gathered, the co-teaching program should be revised. Perhaps some early implementers at an elementary school decide that they want to loop to the next grade with their shared students. In a middle school, changes might be made so that co-teaching is available in social studies as well as English and math. In high school, the reduction in discipline referrals from co-taught classes could lead the planning team to decide to expand the number of co-taught sections being offered. During the early part of implementation, planning team members should ask themselves questions such as these: What parts of our program are working so well that we want to keep them? What dilemmas have been encountered? How can they be resolved? What changes would help our program grow and become integrated into our overall school initiatives to improve student outcomes?

Plan for ongoing support.

As time goes by, co-teaching programs strengthen, but long-range planning still is needed. For example, decisions need to be made about the length of time a partnership should last and what to do if a partner leaves unexpectedly. Long-term goals also should be discussed: Once initial goals are met, what are the goals for sustaining the program? This question could be the most important one of all for programs that are established because it takes several years of focused efforts—even after a program is operating smoothly—to institutionalize it. That is, time is needed for the program to become so much a part of the services in a school that it is not likely to deteriorate because of other normal changes that occur in schools such as staff or administrative turnover. To address sustainability, the planning team might ask questions such as these: How can we ensure that new participants are prepared for co-teaching after start-up training is concluded and no longer routinely offered? What are the dilemmas that often occur in our school that could affect co-teaching? How could we address these? What are examples of other programs that have been sustained? What made them successful and how could we duplicate those results?

Evaluation of Co-Teaching Programs

As you have already learned, evaluation of a co-teaching program should begin prior to the first day that teachers share a lesson. But if you're past the program development phase and have not considered how to evaluate your program, it is still essential that you do so (Idol, 2006; Morocco & Aguilar, 2002). First, evaluating the co-teaching program lets teachers know whether they are having a positive impact on their students and it can suggest directions to take if data indicate changes should be made. Second, program evaluation information can be used to educate parents about co-teaching and its effects on students with disabilities and their typical peers. Third, evaluation data are important to present to the school board or others from whom continued support for co-teaching is necessary.

To accurately judge whether co-teaching as a service delivery option is effective, a two-part process is required. The first is a check to see whether co-teaching has been implemented based on the criteria presented in this book. The second is to evaluate its outcomes. Eventually, evaluation results should be shared with appropriate audiences.

Evaluation of Implementation

Have you ever read a report about co-teaching and realized that a key piece of information was missing—namely, what exactly constituted co-teaching? Before you can evaluate the outcomes of the co-teaching program, you have to know that it actually occurred. In research terms, this is called *fidelity of implementation*. This information is fundamental because you would not expect to see positive results if all that has been implemented is to have a second adult seated in the corner of the classroom. Even in a school with several co-taught classes, the planning team or individual responsible for evaluation should use the checklists and other materials in this handbook to confirm that both teachers are active participants in co-teaching and that instruction has been adjusted as needed to better match student needs (Cook & Friend, 1995).

In new programs, the questions to guide this part of evaluation should be based on the program development goals and overall plan. In programs already established, the core question is this: What has occurred that is being labeled as co-teaching? Examples of specific questions that could be examined and the kinds of evidence that could demonstrate their completion include these:

What training activities have been undertaken to foster collaboration, inclusive practices, and co-teaching?

- Staff development for teachers and administrators (school and district)
  Evidence: announcements of training opportunities, participant logs, training materials, minutes of meetings, copies of newsletters

- Parent education
  Evidence: advertising materials (for example, e-mail announcements, brochures), training materials

- Student education
  Evidence: training materials, copies of activities completed by students related to disability awareness

How has service delivery changed for students with disabilities?

- For how many students with disabilities has the amount of time spent in general education increased?
  Evidence: recorded IEP services, required December 1 child count data

- How much has the amount of time spent in general education increased for each student?
  Evidence: student schedules, IEP records of service delivery

- To what extent has co-teaching been implemented? In which classes? How often? For what periods of time?
  Evidence: teacher schedules, master schedule, teacher reports

- To what extent is classroom co-teaching practice judged to meet criteria for quality?
  Evidence: teacher reports, observational data, checklists

How have instructional practices (academic and behavior) changed?

- To what extent is differentiating occurring?
  Evidence: teacher reports, student materials, observational data, unobtrusive measures (for example, posting of classroom expectations and reward systems)

- How has classroom management changed?
  Evidence: Indicators of the use of positive behavior strategies posted in the classroom, copies of individual student behavior management materials such as contract, notebooks for home communication

This list of program implementation questions and evidence is not exhaustive. It is intended to show you how important it is to check that the program you are evaluating has incorporated some of the key areas that should have a positive impact on students' learning.

The next question is what to do if it appears that the quality of co-teaching is not yet adequate to evaluate it. The straightforward answer is that the planning team should identify the key areas of concern and take specific steps to improve them. In a large district with many implementers this could occur while outcome information is gathered in classrooms or schools where the fidelity of implementation is established. In small schools or districts, program refinements might need to be made before data collection continues.

Evaluation of Outcomes

The second part of evaluation, based on confirmation that co-teaching is being implemented, is to determine its effects. The core question to be asked at this point is the following: What has been the impact of co-teaching? Several questions and examples of evidence can guide this part of the evaluation process:

How has student achievement been influenced by the implemented activities?

Evidence: Longitudinal student achievement data (self-comparison); achievement data from current year for students with disabilities and peers without disabilities in the same school (within-school patterns); achievement data for students with disabilities and students without disabilities from participating schools and comparable non-participating schools (cross-school comparison)

How has student behavior been influenced by the implemented activities?

Evidence: Longitudinal student discipline records for students who have been in a single school for 2-3 years (self-comparison); discipline records from current year for students with disabilities and peers without disabilities in the same school (within-school patterns); discipline records for students with disabilities and students without disabilities from participating schools and comparable non-participating schools (cross-school comparison)

What has been the impact of the initiative's activities on the perceptions of school professionals, parents, and others?

Evidence: Survey or questionnaire results; interview data, anecdotal reports

Several of the items listed above already are gathered at school, including achievement data and behavior records. Some of the information is gathered, but it may need to be supplemented. An example in this area is achievement scores. If only the results of high stakes testing are used to determine co-teaching effectiveness, it may take several years for scores on these once-per-year assessments to change enough that the impact of co-teaching can clearly be seen. In addition, for some students—speaking realistically—test scores may not rise to the level of being considered proficient. In the short term and for some of the students who have the most significant learning difficulty, other types of achievement measures are needed, including curriculum based measures that are a more microscopic look at learning than high stakes tests were ever intended to be.

Gathering data about teachers', parents', and students' perspectives on co-teaching usually requires developing surveys and seeking new data. In the appendix following this chapter sample instruments that could be used or adapted for this purpose are included.

Communication of Results

Evaluation results should be shared with the appropriate audiences. For example, the professionals at a school may decide that they should share both the quantitative and qualitative data they have gathered about co-teaching at a meeting of their school's parent organization or perhaps at the meeting of an advocacy group that supports parents of students with disabilities. Similarly, professionals should consider describing co-teaching impact for members of their school boards. This type of presentation might include a brief summary of data and stakeholder input as well as examples of student successes or even presentations by students who have been in co-taught classes.

In addition, schools and school districts should consider posting data about the co-teaching program on their websites or preparing brochures for distribution that describe the program and its impact on students. These strategies make the information readily accessible to a broader audience, including community members. One other strategy is to ask local media to feature effective inclusive programs for students with disabilities. Co-teaching should be part of that coverage, including data demonstrating its impact on student outcomes and stakeholders' perceptions of it. That is, as program success grows, the news should be shared.

It may seem that making the time for comprehensive program evaluation is time taken away from co-teaching itself. That notion is short-sighted. Evaluation provides you and your colleagues with the information that will keep your co-teaching program evolving and successful. In this era of data-based decision making and accountability, the rationale for evaluating your co-teaching program is even clearer—decisions about what to do next should not be based on opinion—they have to be made based on facts.

For Further Thought

1. If you were going to begin teaching in a new school where teachers had been selected because of their commitment to co-teaching and inclusive practices, what advice would you give to school leaders to ensure that co-teaching got off to a positive start and was able to sustain its success?

2. Professional development is an essential component of program development, but it can occur in many ways. What types of professional development would be helpful at your school? What topics should be addressed? What format would be most effective in increasing professionals' knowledge and skills? What type of professional development is needed by participating co-teachers and which should be offered to all staff members?

3. All the educators in today's schools are busy ensuring that student achievement rises, graduation rates improve, and behavior problems decrease, and they gather data to know how they're doing in those areas. What data would inform you and your colleagues about the impact of co-teaching? What rationale would you offer for the importance of gathering those data?

Taking Action

1. If your school has not started or just begun a co-teaching program, review the steps of program development outlined in this chapter. Identify those that have been completed and those that have not received attention. Using the chart in this chapter's appendix, make a plan with specific steps so that co-teaching is implemented in an effective way.

2. If your co-teaching service has been in place for more than a year, complete an evaluation of it. Gather information on teacher, paraprofessional, administrator, student, and parent perceptions of co-teaching, and collect and analyze student data. Use the results of your evaluation to make a plan for refining or expanding it.

3. If you are still working to firmly establish a co-teaching program that is underway but not yet integral to school services, consider using data to prepare a brief presentation for your school board, a summary of co-teaching for your school's website, or a press release to be shared with local media.

References

Cook, L., & Friend, M. (1995). Co-teaching guidelines for creating effective practices. *Focus on Exceptional Children, 28*(2), 1–12.

Dieker, L. (2007). *Demystifying secondary inclusion: Powerful schoolwide and classroom strategies.* Port Chester, NY: Dude Publishing.

Friend, M., & Pope K. L. (2005). Creating schools in which all students can succeed. *Kappa Delta Pi Record, 41*(2), 56-61.

Hord, S., Rutherford, W., Huling-Austin, L., & Hall, G. (1987). *Taking charge of change.* Alexandria, VA: Association for Supervision and Curriculum Development.

Idol, L. (2006). Toward inclusion of special education students in general education: A program evaluation of eight schools. *Remedial and Special Education, 27,* 77-94.

Morocco, C. C., & Aguilar, C. M. (2002). Coteaching for content understanding: A schoolwide model. *Journal of Educational and Psychological Consultation, 13,* 315-347.

Schlechty, P. C. (2006) On the frontier of school reform with trailblazers, pioneers, and settlers. *The Learning System, 2*(3), 1, 7.

Schwahn, C., & Spady, W. (1998). Why change doesn't happen and how to make sure it does. *Educational Leadership, 55*(7), 45–47.

Villa, R. A., Thousand, J. S., & Nevin, A. I. (2004). *A guide to co-teaching: Practical tips for facilitating student learning.* Thousand Oaks, CA: Corwin.

Waldron, N., & McLeskey, J. (2001). Helping schools include all learners. *Intervention in School and Clinic, 36,* 175-181.

Chapter 6 Appendix

• • • • • •

The first item in this appendix is a simple planning chart that can assist school professionals in developing their co-teaching program. This appendix also contains tools for evaluating co-teaching programs. It includes a survey for special and general education teachers, a survey for parents, and interview questions that could be used to explore students' perceptions of their two-teacher classrooms. These tools are a starting point; you may need to revise them to better suit your school's program, your state's policies, and your information needs.

Action Planning Chart

School _____

Date _____

Task No.	Description	Persons Responsible	Year: J F M A M J J A S O N D	Year: J F M A M J J A S O N D	Year: J F M A M J J A S O N D

170   Chapter 6 Appendix

Co-Teaching Survey: Teachers

The purpose of this survey is to find out what all the people involved in our co-teaching program think about it. Please respond to each of the following items and then return the survey to the box on the counter in the office. Thanks!

General education teacher _____   Special education teacher _____

Grade level/subject _____

I am currently co-teaching: _____ yes   _____ no

Strongly Agree	Agree	Neutral	Disagree	Strongly Disagree		
_____	_____	_____	_____	_____	1.	I understand the purpose/goals of our co-teaching program.
_____	_____	_____	_____	_____	2.	Students learn better in the co-taught classes than they did previously.
_____	_____	_____	_____	_____	3.	Student behavior is better in the co-taught classes than other classes.
_____	_____	_____	_____	_____	4.	Co-teaching is benefiting students with special needs.
_____	_____	_____	_____	_____	5.	Co-teaching is benefiting students at-risk for school failure.
_____	_____	_____	_____	_____	6.	Co-teaching is benefiting average students.
_____	_____	_____	_____	_____	7.	Co-teaching is benefiting gifted/talented students.
_____	_____	_____	_____	_____	8.	Overall, I'm satisfied with the current co-teaching program.

Other comments about program strengths, areas of concern, or requests for information:

Co-Teaching Survey: Parents

The purpose of this survey is to find out what parents of students in classrooms that sometimes have had two teachers this school year think about the program, called co-teaching. Please respond to each of the following items and then return the survey to school with your child in the envelope provided. Thanks!

Child's grade level _____My child receives special education: _____ yes ____ no

Strongly Agree	Agree	Neutral	Disagree	Strongly Disagree	
____	____	____	____	____	1. I understand the purpose and goals of the co-teaching program.
____	____	____	____	____	2. My child has learned better in the co-taught classes than he/she did previously.
____	____	____	____	____	3. My child's behavior is better in the co-taught class than other classes.
____	____	____	____	____	4. Co-teaching is benefiting my child.
____	____	____	____	____	5. Co-teaching is benefiting other students in my child's class(es).
____	____	____	____	____	6. Overall, I'm satisfied with the current co-teaching program.

What comments has your child made regarding the co-teaching program?

What questions or comments do you have about the co-teaching program?

Co-Teaching: Interview or Essay Questions for Students

Although some students—particularly those who are very young and those who have significant intellectual disabilities—might have difficulty articulating their ideas about co-teaching, many students can share their perspectives through an interview. Generally, students should be interviewed in a quiet place by someone with whom they are comfortable. Also, the interviewer should be aware that students might need to be prompted to respond—a question might need to be asked in more than one way or with follow-up. Older students may be asked to write about their perspectives on co-teaching using one or several of these questions.

Here are some sample questions to ask students. The specific vocabulary used should be adjusted to be appropriate for the students interviewed.

1. This year in your classroom (or name subject area) there were sometimes two teachers. What did you think of this?

2. If you think about your classroom with two teachers, what kinds of activities did you do that you did not do when there was only one teacher? What did you think of these activities?

3. What was the best part of having two teachers in the classroom? What parts didn't you like? Why?

4. Why do you think that two teachers were in your classroom? What was each one's job?

5. How did your class with two teachers compare to when you've only had one teacher (in another class or last year)? Why? What's different about the class?

6. How did you do with schoolwork this year in the class with two teachers? Worse than last year? About the same? Better? How do you know?

7. How do you think you behaved this year in the class with two teachers? Worse than last year? About the same? Better? How do you know?

8. Would you like to be in a class with two teachers again? Why or why not?

Chapter 7
Administrative Roles and Responsibilities in Co-Teaching

● ● ● ● ● ●

If your actions inspire others to dream more, learn more, do more and become more, you are a leader.

--John Quincy Adams

Chapter Objectives

1. Summarize key understandings related to co-teaching and your vision for its contribution in educating students with disabilities.

2. Clarify key administrative responsibilities in designing co-teaching programs.

3. Describe personnel matters related to co-teaching, including ways to support co-teachers.

4. Outline ways administrators can ensure that co-teaching programs are effective and efficient.

5. Discuss strategies for communicating with parents and community members about co-teaching.

When teachers are learning about co-teaching or brainstorming strategies to refine their practices, their most common concern is not about the students they teach, the materials they have, or the classrooms where they work. Instead, it concerns administrators. Time and time again, they say, "All this information about co-teaching is fine, but without the support of my principal nothing is going to change at my school." Some teachers call their principals and ask them to join the professional development. Many teachers try to find bits of information they can use in their partnered classroom even without administrative support. A few teachers seem to give up, leaning back in their chairs and viewing the ideas being shared with obvious skepticism.

On the other hand, when administrators are participants in co-teaching professional development, they repeatedly express their strong endorsement of this way of educating students with disabilities. They also note that they provide ongoing support for their co-teachers.

There is no strategy to determine whose perceptions are accurate, and in the end it probably does not matter a great deal. What is striking is that teachers implementing co-teaching believe they are not supported, and their commitment to co-teaching is remarkably different from the commitment expressed by teachers who can identify signals of administrative support. At the same time, this does not mean that administrators are not supportive. What is obvious is that communication is not clear.

As is true with many school initiatives, creating and sustaining co-teaching programs is largely related to the principal's understanding of and commitment to it. And so if you are a principal or assistant principal reading this chapter, thank you for caring enough to take the time (and I hope you have read or plan to read all the other chapters since they contain information essential for you). If you are a teacher looking for information about principal support, perhaps you'll find in these pages some topics that you'll want to share with your principal. And if you are a district administrator such as a curriculum coordinator, special education director, or supervisor, your work in facilitating co-teaching also is important, and you may be able to assist site administrators and teachers in taking the concepts and strategies from discussion to action.

Principals and other school administrators are immensely busy. They arrive at school early, leave late, attend school board meetings in the evenings, address the most serious student issues, and calm upset parents. They make decisions about budget, personnel, and the school's physical plant. They do not hear the words "thank you" nearly often enough. And co-teaching is one more item on the agenda. However, the importance of administrators' direct involvement in all aspects of co-teaching cannot be stressed enough. From meeting the standards set in NCLB to fulfilling the requirements of IDEA to creating opportunities for students to excel, co-teaching can be integral to a school's success—but only if administrators are there to lead.

This chapter extends information presented elsewhere in this handbook with a special emphasis on administrative roles and responsibilities. It examines administrators' understandings of co-teaching and commitment to it, their vision and program design, their management of personnel matters as well as program administration, and also communication beyond the walls of the school.

Personal Understandings and Commitment

In discussing the necessary components of a successful co-teaching program, a teacher made a comment that captures a critical message. She said, "If your principal only knows one paragraph about co-teaching, it's not going anywhere." How true. Before principals and other administrators can lead their schools to develop and implement co-teaching, they first must check their own understandings.

Belief in a Collaborative School Culture

Knowledge about co-teaching is just one piece of the puzzle of leading a school to enhance services for students with disabilities. As outlined in Chapter 1, *Key Concepts for Understanding Co-Teaching*, and emphasized in Chapter 6, *Co-Teaching Program Development and Evaluation*, principals must have a thorough understanding of collaboration. This is essential for several reasons. First, the business of schooling has gotten so complex that collaboration is essential (Barth, 2006; Dufour, 2006). It facilitates the accomplishment of many school initiatives and mandates that lead to student achievement. Even though being an educator in today's schools may be challenging, a culture of collegiality makes achieving what sometimes seems impossible possible.

Second, a collaborative culture is necessary as professionals find ways to meet the needs of their increasingly diverse learners. Two (or three or four or more) heads truly are better than one when the task is to develop innovative ways to reach students.

Third, co-teaching is a highly collaborative service, and so it thrives when set in a culture where collaboration is the norm. That is, when teaching partners are already accustomed to working together, transferring partnership to the classroom is a small step.

Commitment to Inclusive Practices

A second dimension of understanding concerns inclusive practices (Abell, Bauder, & Simmons, 2005). Some principals embrace inclusive practices. They welcome all students into the school, expect teachers to enthusiastically address diverse student needs, and participate with great reluctance in decision-making that removes a student from the general education setting. They often discuss inclusive practices with teachers and other staff members, and they seek information that can help them keep the message of inclusion meaningful.

Other principals have a limited understanding of inclusive practices, or, sadly, they do not subscribe to an inclusive belief system. They may maintain that students who cannot keep up with the standard curriculum should not be placed into classrooms with peers. They may support students with disabilities being in the general education setting, but only if teachers in the school agree with this placement. They sometimes spend a great deal of time discussing what students with disabilities cannot do and bemoaning the expectation that these students now access the general curriculum. They may even make comments like this: "We didn't make AYP last year because of the students with disabilities," implying that if they were not part of the achievement expectations, all would be well. What a very unfortunate viewpoint for a person who is supposed to be an instructional leader to hold.

Without an understanding of and commitment to inclusive practices, co-teaching is not likely to have a positive impact on student achievement. That is not to say that administrators won't have questions about inclusive schools or concerns about the strategies for supporting students with disabilities in the general curriculum—those are expected reactions to schools changing their philosophy about teaching and learning. What is crucial, though, is that administrators reflect on how the strength (or lack thereof) of their beliefs may influence teachers' beliefs and actions. If inclusive thinking is central to a principal's approach to leading a school, it also will be central to the teachers and other staff members.

Understanding of Co-Teaching

The third area of understanding concerns co-teaching itself. Administrators should analyze all the many dimensions of this service delivery option so they are prepared to discuss them with teachers, explain them to parents, and problem solve to address issues that arise. It is surprising how often principals admit that a central office adminstator or special education director told them that effective the following year co-teaching is to be implemented in all schools. They relay the message to special education teachers, ask for general education teachers who would like to volunteer, and then leave the teachers to figure out what they should do. This form of passive acceptance of co-teaching is not at all the same as having a detailed understanding that permits planning to be proactive and problems to be addressed promptly. When principals do not understand co-teaching, it becomes a nice experiment carried out by dedicated individuals, but it also usually stops when those professionals leave the school or move into other positions.

A Clearly Articulated Vision

As administrators grow in their knowledge about collaboration, inclusion, and co-teaching, they should clarify the vision they have of a co-teaching program (Villa, Thousand, & Nevin, 2006). Their vision should be just that—a sweeping view of how the school could provide supports and services to all students. It should relate to students with disabilities, but also should include students who are

English language learners and those who are gifted and talented. A vision about this service is critical not just because it creates a mindset about what is possible over the next several years, but also because it helps to place co-teaching within the larger school context. Ideally, co-teaching should be part of the schools' strategic or improvement planning process.

Unambiguous Message

The administrator's next step in establishing co-teaching is to communicate to teachers and other staff members what the expectations are regarding co-teaching. That is, principals should be clear that as a program begins it will rely on volunteers, but that over time participating in co-teaching or other services in the school is an expectation that comes with the job.

Many strategies can be used to ensure this message is clear. Usually, these strategies are positive. Some principals arrange for their teachers to go on a whole-day retreat to renew their commitment to teaching all students and working with colleagues in the classroom. Some principals ensure that co-teachers have extra opportunities to attend conferences or visit other co-teaching programs. Yet others offer general encouragement, but they also arrange for private meetings when particular teachers are reluctant participants. One principal was faced with several teachers in a grade level refusing to participate in co-teaching. After providing time for the teachers to visit other classes, discussing the importance with them as a group, and individually advising them that co-teaching would be implemented—it was not a choice, the principal involuntarily transferred two of the teachers to a different grade level. This step seems harsh, but the message was clear and after very appropriate assistance had been provided to the teachers, the principal was left with no other option.

A high school principal used a completely different approach. In the third year of his program, he let general education teachers know that all teachers working with students in advanced placement courses would automatically also be scheduled to work in a co-taught class. His decision clearly conveyed that all teachers are responsible for all students, regardless of their seniority or teaching preferences.

Visible Reminders

Principals and other administrators can ensure that all professionals understand that co-teaching is a priority by creating visible signals of it. They can order name plates that have both teachers' names on them for partnerships that exist for most of the school day. They can address co-teaching in their weekly communication with teachers and in their meetings with grade levels, teams, or departments. They can ask co-teachers to give updates on their practices at faculty meetings. When principals discuss achievement data, outcomes for co-taught classes can be disaggregated and presented as a means of indicating their impact on student learning. Finally, principals can provide to all teachers snippets of information—brief articles from the professional literature, websites, print materials from professional conferences— on improving co-teaching practices. The point of these reminders is to help all teachers integrate co-teaching into their thinking about their roles and responsibilities as professionals.

Effective and Efficient Program Design

Principals have a perspective on the overall operation of a school that can help to guide the development of co-teaching. For example, they are aware of some of the idiosyncrasies of scheduling and the dilemmas of arranging common planning time. They also have a sense of how to distribute students across classrooms or sections.

Principals also can help teachers see that some options for co-teaching are unlikely to be ideal. For example, in some middle and high schools special educators spend just 20 or 25 minutes in a classroom and then race to another one, sometimes showing up in three courses in a single block-scheduled class period. Other co-teachers decide, probably in an attempt to be equitable, to alternate between classes during a single class period. Of course, the problem is that they walk into each class for each session not knowing what occurred the day before.

Principals can address other program design matters as well. For example, elementary special educators may feel pressured to provide more services to students (in general education and in special education) than there are minutes available, and so they give up their lunch and planning time. Principals should ensure these essential breaks are kept in schedules. Principals also can arrange for all co-teachers to periodically get together so that they can compare notes, enjoy their successes, brainstorm about dilemmas, and consider refinements for the program going forward. They encourage teachers to gather appropriate data and they lead discussions of the impact of co-teaching on student achievement. Collectively, principals should lead all the aspects of program development and evaluation outlined in Chapter 6.

Personnel and Support for Them

In some ways, the most important role of a principal in implementing co-teaching is addressing matters related to personnel. The purpose of co-teaching, of course, is to educate students with disabilities, but the key to its success is the people who implement it.

Hiring New Teachers

A starting point for addressing personnel matters is to make a firm commitment to recommend for hire only teachers who understand that co-teaching is a likely job responsibility. Principals should go far beyond asking whether candidates are supportive of inclusive practices. They should pose problems, relying on experiences at the school from the current or a preceding year, to see how the prospective teachers would respond. The key is to look for professionals who welcome opportunities to work with colleagues in the classroom and who are willing to change some of their practices as a natural part of forming such a partnership.

Assigning Partners

After the stage in program development where co-teachers are volunteers, principals should assume responsibility for assigning teaching partners in schools where many options exist. One strategy is to ask teachers to write down two or three preferences for co-teachers and then to make decisions on that basis. However partners are assigned, principals should try to notify them before the end of the school year, or, if that is not possible, as soon as possible during the summer. One very unreasonable strategy is to tell special educators at the beginning of the school year who they are to teach with and then send them to those teachers to tell them the news. This handing off of responsibility communicates more loudly than any words a lack of administrative commitment.

Observing Implementation

Principals should plan to observe co-teachers, both as part of their supervision responsibilities and as a means of judging co-teaching effectiveness. An observation generally can use the same format as other teacher observations. Teachers should provide their shared lesson plan and an overview of their plan for co-teaching. The principal should observe the lesson, noting the relationship between the teachers, the quality of the instruction, and the intensity applied in meeting student needs. After the observation, the principal should check with teachers for their perspectives on the lesson and ask additional questions about their shared work. A template for observing co-teachers is included in the appendix that follows this chapter.

Arranging Professional Development

Time and again, teachers report that they are co-teaching but have never participated in professional development related to it. Principals can nurture teaching partners' effectiveness by arranging for them to receive appropriate preparation for this type of teaching. In districts where personnel turnover is small, continuous attention to professional development may not be necessary. However, in urban districts where turnover is high and hiring for the school year may still be occurring as students are arriving, professional development should be an ongoing option. Initial training, whether in a face-to-face format or through an on-line course, should be followed by coaching, feedback, and opportunities for discussions and visits to classrooms with established practices (Salend, Gordon, & Lopez-Vona, 2002). As noted in Chapter 6, *Co-Teaching Program Development and Evaluation*, preparing professionals to co-teach is critical.

Addressing Resistance

Despite careful hiring and focused professional development, some teachers may be resistant to co-teaching. Special educators sometimes report that they are told by general educators that they should sit quietly while instruction occurs and then help the students who did not understand. General educators sometimes say that special educators just will not take any initiative, that they are perfectly happy to sit quietly or frequently volunteer to take students with disabilities to a separate setting for "extra help." In other situations, teachers may state that they do not want to co-teach.

Principals and other administrators who work with co-teachers have a strong obligation to facilitate the difficult conversations that can get resistance out into the open and possibly reduce or eliminate it. It is easy to think that teachers should be professional enough to be able to do this themselves, but the fact is that in many cases they cannot. Special educators may feel as though they must have permission for their classroom activities. General educators may be frustrated by special educators' reticence. Principals can speak to each educator separately, observe the co-teaching practices, meet with both teachers, and carefully facilitate sessions to help the teachers negotiate their relationship.

Problem Solving When Dilemmas Occur

When teachers are frustrated because a student in the co-taught class is having serious behavior problems, principals should be part of the conversation to help them strategize and develop ways to determine if their ideas are effective in addressing the problem. When one co-teacher goes to the principal to express dissatisfaction about the other, principals should follow up by seeking input from the second teacher and then arranging to speak to the teachers when they can be together.

Problem solving describes much of what a principal does on a day-to-day basis (Gray, 2006), and it is a key strategy for nurturing co-teaching. And if solutions are not easily found, the principal can at least sympathize over the situation, help generate ideas for ameliorating the situation as much as possible, and promise resolution for the following year or semester.

Program Administration

Some administrators put a great deal of effort into developing a co-teaching program, staffing it, and assigning students to it. Eventually, though, their attention is drawn to other pressing matters—achievement scores hitting a plateau, a newly mandated reading program, a series of serious behavior incidents. Co-teaching is not so much ignored as moved far down on the priority list. In a few cases, this change is not significant. Highly competent teachers manage the day-to-day operation of the program, parents are satisfied, and student achievement improves.

However, especially during the initial five or six years, co-teaching programs are somewhat fragile and likely to need ongoing input and monitoring from principals and other administrators. If you remember that co-teaching is antithetical to the professional preparation of many teachers, the reason for this continued support becomes clear. Most teachers learned through their student teaching experiences that when they really achieved success they would be working primarily alone, at least for instruction. Co-teaching is premised on sharing a classroom in a highly collaborative way. Expecting all the partnerships and the logistics to easily fall into place is not realistic. Teachers may need continued coaching, parents may continue to seek information, students may have questions, and logistical problems may arise without warning. The level of support may not be intense, but continued attention should be incorporated into long-range plans.

Principals and other administrators could make a checklist of program administration responsibilities by reading the material presented throughout this handbook. Those are the tasks that may require attention, and teachers may be able to generate a few additional areas for principal input. The message is this: Co-teaching programs generally do not self-sustain; strong leadership is required.

Communication Beyond the School

Principals and other administrators have a key responsibility to ensure that communication about co-teaching (and other inclusive practices) is detailed and accurate. They can accomplish this through several strategies.

Website Information

If co-teaching is an integral part of special education throughout a school district, information about it should be included on the district website in a location that can be accessed by anyone interested in the topic. That is, it should not be included only on a page that includes items dealing with students with disabilities. However, if a district description of this service is not available, school websites definitely should communicate its existence. One suggestion for doing this is to include co-teaching on the same webpage where a variety of school programs are summarized. That is, a school may have an after-school tutoring program, literacy coaches who model lessons in elementary classrooms, after-school test preparation workshops, or peer tutoring. Co-teaching likewise should be listed as a means of enhancing student achievement. The rationale for presenting information in this way is to clearly describe co-teaching, but to do so in a way that conveys it as a support that is integral to the school, not a special event that should cause parents and others to question it.

Letters to Parents

Teachers sometimes ask whether a letter should be sent home to parents at the beginning of the school year explaining that co-teaching is occurring. Although certainly there are exceptions to any advice offered, I usually discourage this practice. Most typical learners have had classmates with disabilities throughout their school careers; that is nothing new. The only change is that the classroom is gaining an extra teacher. If too great an emphasis is placed on the addition of a teacher, parent anxiety may be unnecessarily heightened.

In some schools, a decision is made that a letter should be sent home, but it is prepared by the principal. This more general type of letter can communicate the same information that teachers would share, but do so with an authority and tone that teachers cannot convey. This approach also suggests that questions about the program should be communicated to the principal, thus taking stress for responding away from the teachers.

Parent Concerns

Another responsibility for principals and other administrators is addressing parent concerns about co-teaching. Parents of students with disabilities may like the small, structured environment in which their children have been educated. They may be reluctant to agree that their children would benefit from the general education classroom and instruction provided there. If the students in question are in high school and have never participated in general education classes, this perspective is understandable and should be respected. But if the students are younger, principals can help parents to understand that this option may provide opportunities students have never before had. Although the decision about placement is clearly the responsibility of the IEP team, principals can offer insights about the benefits of co-teaching as a special education service and can suggest a short-term trial with agreement to reconvene the team and revise the IEP if necessary.

Parents of students who do not have disabilities may presume that curriculum in a co-taught class is watered down. Principals should listen respectfully to this parent perspective, ask about the basis for it, and clarify that this notion is rather common but untrue. If parents want to dictate which classes their children are assigned to, principals should avoid being swayed by this parent pressure. Finally, if parents have a legitimate concern (for example, a student with a disability is hitting their children on the bus), the principal, of course, should investigate and address the situation appropriately.

Strong principals express their commitment to co-teaching and set expectations for teachers. They demonstrate their commitment by providing specific supports for co-teaching (including professional development and time for shared planning), and they proactively work to address logistical and interpersonal problems that may arise. They know the students with disabilities and monitor their assessment results to ensure their services are effective. More than anything, they care deeply about every child in their schools, and they help their teachers to celebrate all the student successes they achieve (Burrello, Beatty, & Lashley, 2003). The job is daunting, and being able to leap over tall buildings might help. Ultimately, though, it is a principal's leadership that determines how successful and sustainable co-teaching programs will be.

For Further Thought

1. What do you think are the three most important actions a principal can take to foster the growth of an effective co-teaching program?

2. How should a principal respond when a co-teacher reports that the other educator is unwilling to create a classroom partnership (either the special educator or the general educator)? How do you think the response of teachers and administrators will vary in addressing this dilemma?

3. Principals and other administrators sometimes are assisted by having scripts—comments they have already thought through—for responding to parent concerns about co-teaching. What are the scripts that should be the basis for responding to concerns of parents at your schools?

Taking Action

1. Request that co-teaching be a topic for discussion at a principal's meeting. Plan an agenda that includes items such as the level of district commitment to co-teaching, resources allocated, and co-teaching as related to district or school strategic planning.

2. Review your school's website. What programs and services are listed on it? How could co-teaching be added to this listing? Prepare a webpage that captures the key details of your school's co-teaching program.

3. Plan a presentation about co-teaching for your parent organization. Consider including a summary of data demonstrating the impact co-teaching has on student outcomes, testimonials from current co-teachers, and stories about students—told by teachers, told by students, or (for older students) written by students.

References

Abell, M. M., Bauder, D. K., & Simmons, T. J. (2005). Access to the general curriculum: A curriculum and instruction perspective for educators. *Intervention in School and Clinic, 41,* 82-86.

Barth, R. S. (2006). Improving relationships within the schoolhouse. *Educational Leadership,* 53(6), 8-13.

Burrello, L. C., Beatty, E. E., & Lashley, C. (2003). *Educating all students together: How school leaders create unified systems.* Thousand Oaks, CA: Corwin.

Dufour, R. (2006). Collaboration is the key to unlocking potential. *The Learning Principal, 2*(3), 1, 6-7.

Gray, C. (2006). Pulling together: Principals can empower teams of teachers by taking on the role of facilitator. *The Learning Principal, 2*(2), 1, 6-7.

Thousand, J. S., Villa, R. A., & Nevin, A. (2006). What special education administrators need to know about co-teaching. *InCASE, 47*(6), 1-3, 5.

Salend, S. J., Gordon, J., & Lopez-Vona, K. (2002). Evaluating cooperative teaching teams. *Intervention in School and Clinic, 37,* 195-200.

Chapter 7 Appendix

● ● ● ● ● ●

The observation form on the following pages was designed to address these common administrative questions about co-teaching: What should I be looking for when I observe a co-taught class? On what basis should I judge the quality of the co-teaching that I'm seeing?

A Template for Observing the Implementation of Co-Teaching

Teachers _____   Date _____

_____   School _____

Subject _____   Lesson _____

Information Gathered Before Observation

Objectives/Setting Notes

_____

_____

Topics for Feedback Requested by the Teachers

_____

_____

_____   Lesson plan that explains implementation of co-teaching

_____   Information (as needed) on students with disabilities in the class

Information Gathered During Observation

NOTES

1. One or more specific approaches for co-teaching, or a variation of them, are in use.

    Novice   *1*   *2*   *3*   *4*   *5*   *Expert*

2. Instruction is well-organized.

    Novice   *1*   *2*   *3*   *4*   *5*   *Expert*

3. The teachers interact with each other during instruction in ways that further the instructional goals of the lesson.

    Novice   *1*   *2*   *3*   *4*   *5*   *Expert*

4. The lesson is based on principles of active learning.

    Novice   *1*   *2*   *3*   *4*   *5*   *Expert*

5. Both the curricular content and the processes of learning are incorporated into instruction.

    Novice   *1*   *2*   *3*   *4*   *5*   *Expert*

6. Both teachers show evidence of making teaching accommodations based on student needs.

    Novice   *1*   *2*   *3*   *4*   *5*   *Expert*

7. Print and other instructional materials and activities show evidence of accommodations for students' special needs.

    Novice   *1*   *2*   *3*   *4*   *5*   *Expert*

8. Instructional intensity is greater than would be possible with only one teacher present.

    Novice   *1*   *2*   *3*   *4*   *5*   *Expert*

9. Both teachers are involved in checking student learning.

    Novice   *1*   *2*   *3*   *4*   *5*   *Expert*

10. Evidence of parity is present in the classroom.

    Novice   *1*   *2*   *3*   *4*   *5*   *Expert*

11. The teachers share responsibilites for classroom management

    Novice   *1*   *2*   *3*   *4*   *5*   *Expert*

12. Both teachers respond to student requests for assistance.

    Novice   *1*   *2*   *3*   *4*   *5*   *Expert*

13. Students ask both teachers for assistance.

    Novice   *1*   *2*   *3*   *4*   *5*   *Expert*

14. Students interact appropriately with both teachers.

    Novice   *1*   *2*   *3*   *4*   *5*   *Expert*

15. Both teachers address student behavior/discipline matters.

    Novice   *1*   *2*   *3*   *4*   *5*   *Expert*

16. Transitions between activities occur with a minimum loss of time

    Novice   *1*   *2*   *3*   *4*   *5*   *Expert*

Questions to Explore After Observation

1. How typical was this lesson compared with all your co-taught lessons?

2. How is the classroom different when two teachers are present compared to when only one teacher is here?

3. What accommodations and modifications are being made so that students with disabilities can access the general curriculum?

4. How are you addressing students' IEP goals (and objectives) within co-taught lessons?

5. What are the next steps you plan to take to enrich your knowledge of co-teaching and further its implementation?

Chapter 8
Questions and Concerns about Co-Teaching

● ● ● ● ● ●

It is better to know some of the questions than all of the answers.

–James Thurber

Chapter Objectives

1. Outline co-teaching questions that involve teachers' partnerships and ideas for resolving them.

2. Identify co-teaching questions that relate to program structure and strategies for addressing them.

3. Clarify co-teaching questions related to students' educational needs and parents' concerns and suggestions for dealing with them.

One goal of this book is to address common questions related to co-teaching, and I hope the pages you have already reviewed have addressed many of your concerns. However, in working with teachers, administrators, and other professionals across the country, there are some questions and concerns that span several of the areas covered in the preceding chapters or that seem to need special emphasis. That is the purpose of this chapter. In the following sections you will find questions raised by educators from almost every state and some thoughts on each of them. Many of the responses are based on knowledge gained through experience in schools rather than a specific research study. Some of the topics may not apply to your situation at all, but others may be exactly the concern that you have. Some of the questions are particularly applicable to elementary, middle, or high schools, and others may span grade levels. If you have not found information on a specific issue elsewhere in this manual, perhaps you will find what you're looking for here. Keep in mind that each of these quesions could have several answers, and you might find that you would respond differently. I might respond somewhat differently, too, if the number of pages that could be devoted to each was limitless.

This chapter is organized in three parts. In the first part, concerns about the partnership between teachers are addressed, and in the second part questions about co-teaching program structure and logistics are included. The final section includes items related to students, families, and the delivery of special education services.

Questions and Concerns about Teacher's Partnerships

Many of the questions that arise concerning co-teaching relate to the working relationships teachers develop and the difficulties they encounter in sustaining partnerships. As you consider the questions in this section, what should be more striking than anything is the importance of fostering collaboration as a foundation for co-teaching success.

How should we handle the situation when there is a substitute teacher for one of us?

If one of you needs to be out of school for just a day or a few days, you might decide that the teacher who remains at school should lead instruction while the substitute teacher assists specific students or manages a simple activity based on the co-teaching approaches. That is, expecting a substitute teacher who is there on a temporary basis to immediately be prepared for what, to you, may have become second nature, probably is not realistic. However, if one co-teacher is going to be absent for several weeks, the remaining teacher should meet with the substitute, provide a sort of crash course in co-teaching and the operation of the co-taught class, and expect to continue co-teaching, even if it is with a slightly lower level of skill and commitment.

My co-teacher and I don't have a lot of planning time, and that is not going to change. I could manage if I had the lesson plans in advance, but my co-teacher just doesn't give them to me. She says she usually doesn't write them up until right before instruction. Now what?

Not having the information needed to prepare for teaching can be frustrating, but it also can become a legal issue. That is, the special educator is charged with ensuring that students with disabilities are receiving the instruction they need and the accommodations that will facilitate their learning. Without having lesson plans, it becomes nearly impossible to deliver those services.

The first step in addressing this matter usually is a conversation. The special educator should note the problem and request a solution using words such as these: "I'm very concerned about how we're meeting the needs of the students with disabilities in our class, especially addressing IEP goals. I need lesson plans in advance in order to do my part. What options could we try so that I could have at least a day to prepare?"

Of course, the special educator has to be willing to compromise. It would be nice to receive lesson plans a week in advance, but that may not be possible. Ultimately, if this dilemma is interfering with the delivery of special education services, it may become a matter needing input from an administrator as discussed in Chapter 7.

I'm co-teaching in middle school and struggling to keep up with the curriculum. Sometimes my teaching partner asks me to teach something "on the spot"—no warning, no preparation. Then she uses my discomfort as proof that special educators shouldn't be in general education classrooms. What should I do?

The first step in understanding this situation is to think about the general educator's reason for asking the special educator to teach extemporaneously. Even though it sounds like a form of resistance, it could be the teacher is poorly prepared and often does the same thing. It also could be a matter of realizing the special educator has not led instruction in awhile and really should, but does not think through the discomfort this well-intentioned behavior causes. In other words, the thinking behind this awkward situation may be benign.

Whatever the motive for the general education teacher's actions, being proactive might help. For example, the special education teacher might mention during a planning session that she appreciates the general educator's awareness of the need for her to lead instruction, but that she is not yet comfortable enough with the content to lead without time to prepare. She could then suggest that either they could designate particular lessons coming up in which she might take a lead, or she could suggest that they try one of the co-teaching approaches that could help on this issue. Perhaps they could team, with the special educator interjecting examples and clarifying vocabulary for students. Perhaps they could team for a brief large-group lesson and then divide the students into stations with each teacher working with a group of students on an application or discussion of the day's material. This matter should be addressed sooner rather than later to avoid establishing patterns in the co-taught class that are difficult to change.

Through strong support and careful planning by my principal, my co-teacher and I have weekly shared planning time. However, he usually comes to it late and occasionally never shows up at all. Now what?

When one co-teacher occasionally misses a planning session, it probably is the result of a particularly hectic day, a crisis, or a miscommunication—and should not be a source of concern. However, if shared planning time is allocated but not being used, then it becomes a matter of accountability, and it also could become a threat to co-teaching program integrity. As you might suspect, the teacher who shows up on time probably will have to begin the conversation that addresses this matter. He might note that the scheduled planning time does not seem to be working out very well. The next step is to listen to the response of the other professional. Perhaps having planning time right after students have lunch is causing a problem. In a large high school, it might be the location for the planning—by the time the person who is late wraps up the preceding class, gathers materials, and walks to the planning location (being stopped repeatedly along the way), being late is almost inevitable.

Like nearly all the topics in this section, a conversation is critical. If the reason for the issue can be identified, then perhaps the planning time can be changed, the start time delayed by 10 minutes (to allow for getting there), or the location changed. If the co-teachers are experienced, perhaps they could meet every other week instead of every week and the alternate week used to address some of the matters interfering with planning. This problem also could be one where input from others is helpful. If other teachers also have shared planning time, they may have suggestions on how to ensure it is used.

Finally, mention must be made of the focus for the planning. The teacher who comes late or misses the planning session may not perceive that the time is being used wisely. If that is the case, the teachers probably should clarify their expectations, state their agenda, and renew their commitment to this critical aspect of co-teaching.

I'm ready! I'd like to try as many new ideas as possible to enhance co-teaching, but my partner seems to be completely happy to keep things as they are, which is not really co-teaching at all, and doesn't want to try anything new — she teaches, I wait until the students begin an independent assignment, and then I walk around and assist. What should I do?

When one half of the partnership is reluctant, co-teaching tends to stagnate. Addressing this issue requires your willingness to raise the topic and use effective communication skills to discuss options. Exactly what you say depends partly on whether you are the general educator or the special educator or specialist. However, a first step in knowing how to respond is trying to understand the other person's point of view.

If you are the general educator working with a reluctant special educator, consider that professional's perspective. Is the person uncomfortable with the content? Fearful of making a mistake and of what your reaction might be? Intimidated by your level of content knowledge and skill? Concerned that you consider the classroom yours and might be put off with another professional's input? You could try several conversation starters to allay these concerns and enhance co-teaching. For example, you might say something like this: "I've been reading about co-teaching and ways it can look. Next week I'd like to try something new." Then offer your idea of a new approach to try or a new way to assign roles in the classroom. One specific recommendation is to gauge your suggestion on the comfort level of the other educator. If you sense the reluctance is because of lack of content knowledge, you might propose dividing students during a review but not for initial instruction. If you sense the reluctance is because of overall concern about being in the general education setting, you might propose station teaching, an option that puts students into relatively small groups and permits each teacher to deliver the same instruction three times.

If you are a special educator working with a reluctant general educator, your analysis of the situation might be a bit different. Does the general educator perceive that you are judging the quality of his teaching? Believe that students with disabilities should be in general education settings only if they can keep up with the already-established instructional content and activities? Sense that your presence interferes with the instructional flow and your input results in slowing down the pace of instruction and the ability to cover all the required content?

As advised for general educators, your response should take into account your understanding of the other person's point of view. Depending on your situation, you might raise the topic in this way: "I'm concerned about our co-teaching. I know others are expecting us to raise student achievement but also to meet special needs. I'm not sure what we're doing right now will lead to those results, but I have a couple of ideas we might try." As in the other scenario, it is important to suggest an idea that addresses the other professional's comfort level, perhaps starting with you taking notes on the overhead while the other person delivers a brief lecture or proposing that you do the warm-up activity at the beginning of the class or the wrap-up activity at its conclusion.

Regardless of your role, you should try at least three times to raise the topic and explore ways to address it. If none of your efforts are successful, you might try to involve a colleague who could provide informal input or ask for a meeting for all co-teachers so that ideas can be shared—and perhaps implemented by the reluctant participant. Your last resort, and one that may have serious negative repercussions, is to ask your co-teacher to meet with you and an administrator. This strategy usually reflects that your discomfort has grown to an intolerable level and that you believe students are not getting the education to which they are entitled.

Questions and Concerns about Co-Teaching Program Structure and Logistics

Because each school has a set of unique characteristics that affect the options for arranging co-teaching, shared planning time, and student assignment to classes, the number of issues that arise related to co-teaching program structure and logistics should not be surprising (Walther-Thomas, 1997). These are some of the most common questions about setting up co-teaching programs in a way that makes them integral to the overall school schedule and feasible in terms of most effectively and efficiently utilizing personnel resources.

In our elementary school, all the reading/language arts instruction occurs in the morning, and co-teaching needs to occur in that subject area in several classrooms. As a general education teacher, I don't think the students are getting the support they need because the special educator goes to a different classroom and I cannot reach everyone by myself. I know the special education teachers are frustrated, too, because they can't be everywhere at once. How could we get this scheduled to work better?

When elementary school scheduling is set up in this manner, the first year of a co-teaching program usually highlights the impossibility of offering services to all students entitled to them during such a constricted window of time. This dilemma is particularly difficult because nearly all students with disabilities need services in the areas of reading and language arts.

The solution to this dilemma is to stagger reading/language arts instruction so that it occurs at different times of the day in different grade levels. For example, the kindergarten and first grade teachers may begin the day with this instruction, while the second and third grade teachers begin at mid-morning, and the fourth and fifth grade teachers begin right after lunch. In some schools a pattern like this is used in the fall to take into account the importance of teaching reading to the young children when they first arrive at school. In the spring, however, the order in which the instruction begins may be reversed. This takes into account the upper grade teachers' preference for teaching reading and language arts in the morning.

If teachers and administrators set aside traditional thinking about school scheduling, they often can find a resolution to this issue that is workable for everyone. The results are that services improve and students benefit.

Our model of co-teaching is based on being in classrooms every other day. On the day I'm not in the room, the paraprofessional is there. (Note: This arrangement sometimes occurs in an am/pm rotation, too, where the professional is in one room in the morning and the other in the afternoon and the paraprofessional is in the room where the special educator is not.) It's not working very well. What do you suggest to make the instruction more effective?

Although co-teaching arrangements set up in this manner and supplemented by paraprofessional support can work, often they result in the special educator not ever feeling like he knows what is happening in the general education classroom. Generally, a pattern for services in a general education classroom that takes into account the needs of students and the demands of the curriculum is more appropriate, and many solutions can be generated. For example, one possibility is for the special education teacher to spend Monday, Tuesday, and Wednesday in the first classroom because the students' needs are greater and the most intensive instruction occurs on those days. The paraprofessional supports that classroom later in the week for review and assessment while the special educator co-teaches in the classroom the paraprofessional had supported earlier in the week. In middle schools when the special educator is assigned to the team, the amount of time in each classroom could be negotiated in two-week blocks. That is, if a teacher does not need the support, the co-teacher moves to the other classroom. The only caution is to be certain that IEP goals are addressed and students' time for receiving special education is met.

Overall, this question conveys that a program is based on scheduling patterns instead of student needs. Educators who realize this type of approach is not working should suggest a meeting of all key participants to generate alternatives. It should be noted, too, that this is an opportunity to raise the matter of paraprofessional support. If that individual is not needed in the assigned classroom, perhaps the individual's time could be better spent in another classroom.

I am a special educator who co-teaches nearly fulltime. However, whenever a general education teacher is absent I'm told to cancel co-teaching to cover that teacher's class. Is this appropriate?

Professionals generally understand that if a flu epidemic is spreading across the community and substitute teachers cannot be found, any available professional may be called to help ensure that the educational process is not disrupted for students. However, such situations should be rare, not common. If special educators are asked nearly every week to divert their attention from providing services to students to substitute teach, both legal and ethical issues should be raised. First, each time co-teaching does not occur, students with disabilities are being denied the services to which they are entitled based on their IEPs. A pattern of failure to deliver services because of re-assigning the special educator to other responsibilities could result in liability.

An ethical concern should be mentioned as well. What does this practice say about the value of the co-teaching partnership? Is it a message that the presence of the second professional in the classroom is so limited in impact that it is more important to have that person cover another class? Is it a strategy of convenience— that is, is it easier to re-assign the special educator than to distribute the students to other classes? Whatever the thinking behind this decision, it is a topic that should be raised with a sympathetic administrator and directly discussed. Untenured and early career professionals may not feel they can risk broaching this topic, and so it may fall to experienced, tenured professionals to do this.

Our school has block scheduling. The special education teachers have to spend half the block in one class and half in another. Is this a reasonable expectation?

The answer to this question depends on the needs of the students and other variables related to overall co-teaching program structure. For example, if students with learning disabilities have relatively mild needs and this is a strategy for providing limited assistance in science and social studies, then it may be a reasonable expectation. Similarly, if this is a means of serving students in the

12th grade as part of helping them transition to post-school options, then it may be appropriate. However, if all co-teaching is scheduled in this manner without considering students' needs or curriculum demands, then it could be a problem.

In some cases, the underlying concern is the fact that the special educator is always arriving in one class halfway through instruction and finding that the time is not well spent. If that is the problem, then perhaps the teachers should meet to discuss other options. Could the schedule vary by week in terms of first half, second half? By the topics being address in the classes? By unit? Two principles are guiding this response: Although full-period co-teaching is preferred, sometimes other factors lead to a justifiable reason for it to be a half-block (however, co-teaching for half of a traditional class period is usually not appropriate). At the same time, decisions regarding this matter should be based on student needs and the nature of the instruction.

At our elementary school, we begin the year with everything set up and all students receiving their services. But we have a lot of transience, and so students move in and get placed in classes without co-teaching. Also, we usually identify a number of students during the year, and they're often in classes without co-teaching. How do we make sure they get their special education services?

What is described in this question is perhaps the most common scheduling dilemma of elementary schools. No ideal answer exists, but strategies such as these can reduce the size of this problem:

- If a student is identified as having a disability during the first couple of weeks of the school year, in some situations it might be possible to re-assign the student to the class in which co-teaching is already occurring.

- Special educators in schools where this problem occurs every year should design their schedules with this dilemma in mind, keeping several slots of time open to accommodate the students who move into the district and those identified during the course of the school year. This time can be used for assessment, observation, and short-term support until needed for co-teaching.

- Some students' services may have to be in a pullout environment for the remainder of the school year in which they are identified. This time would come from one of the slots noted above. Alternatively, special educators might blend some of their services so that, if a student needs instruction at a particular time, the special educator who is available at that time provides it even if she is not the student's case manager. Notice that this solution requires special educators to collaborate in designing their services.

We're in the third year of our co-teaching program. Our principal has based co-teaching on volunteers, and next year none of the general education teachers who were asked want to participate. What happens if no one volunteers?

In Chapter 7, the point is made that administrators should clearly articulate the expectation that as co-teaching becomes part of a school's service delivery options, any teacher in the school may be a participant. This question illustrates exactly why this message is so important. If co-teaching is effective for students, then it is offered. It is not really a matter of whether teachers are volunteering. Even though that sounds harsh, basing services on teachers' preferences cannot be justified legally or ethically.

The underlying question that might need to be addressed is why so much reluctance is being encountered. Are too many students with special needs being assigned to a single classroom? Is the support offered to the students and teachers appropriate? If the professionals work to understand the factors leading to this difficult situation, then the likelihood of addressing them and finding workable solutions rises dramatically.

As I observe co-teachers in my school, I'm beginning to notice a problem. Some co-teachers (and this can be either special education or general education teachers) feel free to arrive for class late, apparently because another teacher is there. A few special educators are starting to use co-teaching time to take care of other responsibilities; they're not in the classes where they are supposed to be. As a principal, how should I address these issues?

If you are noticing a pattern, then it may be time to do a bit of investigating. If a check of the program and teachers' schedules indicate that not enough time has been allocated for responsibilities outside the classroom, a solution is to build such time into the schedule so that it is not taken away from co-teaching.

In some cases, this problem indicates that the teachers have not yet created a partnership strong enough that the absence of either teacher is considered a strong obstacle to effective teaching. If this reflects the situation, then a meeting with the two teachers is in order. Alternatively, if one teacher is violating expectations for responsibilities and accountability, then an individual meeting is in order.

Ultimately, co-teachers generally should be in their shared classrooms as assigned. Supporting teachers to understand this, particularly in new programs, is recommended, but this also may become a supervisory matter where an expectation for correcting the problem is appropriate.

Our school has self-contained special education classes as well as co-teaching. Does implementing co-teaching mean we should do away with all separate special education classes?

Not at all. This relates to the topic of inclusion discussed in Chapter 1. In some schools, the terms *inclusion* and *co-teaching* become synonyms, and then professionals may begin stating that their goal is *full inclusion*, actually meaning all students assigned to general education on a fulltime basis with co-teaching as a service. As the terms become mingled the understanding of effective practices decreases.

Federal special education law clearly requires that a full continuum of services be available for students with disabilities. Inclusive schools often have fewer pullout services than other schools, and some schools may not need traditional self-contained classes. However, even in highly inclusive schools some students may require instruction in a separate setting, and that option must be available for them (although in small school districts it may not be available at each school site). Remember, decisions about the appropriate services and placement for students with disabilities must be made on an individual basis, and these decisions are made by the team that writes each student's IEP.

I'm assigned to co-teach in seven classrooms each day. Nothing that I do sounds like what co-teaching is supposed to be. Is it possible to co-teach in this number of places?

When staffing and the way students are assigned to classes create this dilemma, it is time to step back to re-assess the entire program structure. First, this may have occurred because of students being identified or moving in during the course of the school year, and it might be best to have some students receive services in the special education setting for the remainder of the year. Second, this could have resulted because of a decision related to the initial assignment of students to classes. That is, a principal may have decided that in order to be "fair," students would be distributed across all classrooms. Third, this could have resulted when scheduling was managed through computer software without taking into account the need for co-taught sections.

This problem can be avoided by addressing its source. In the meantime, here are some other thoughts on this topic. Usually, special educators who are co-teaching can do so in one or two classes or sections their first year, eventually increasing the number to three or four sections as programs evolve and responsibilities change. Occasionally, a special educator even manages a fifth assignment. However, when the number of classes assigned for co-teaching is as high as seven, a more realistic way of looking at the services is to decide which ones are really another form of service and deliver it accordingly. That is, one of the classes may actually need only consultative support, and this should be offered. Another class may need periodic support and not a partnership. Special educators in this situation should actively discuss this topic with their administrators, looking forward to the next semester or school year to make decisions about how to structure the co-teaching program.

As a special educator in an inclusive school, I feel like I can't do it all. I'm supposed to co-teach in several classes, pull students for remedial instruction, keep up with all the paperwork, attend meetings (that seem to get scheduled when I'm supposed to be co-teaching), communicate with parents, and do anything else that comes along. Do others feel this way?

Yes, they do. One reason why careful and measured program development and ongoing professional development is integral to sustaining co-teaching relates directly to this concern. Co-teaching requires adjustments on the part of all educators, and for special educators, those adjustments can be significant. Feeling overwhelmed can be particularly stressful when programs move quickly from traditional formats to innovative ones. The sense of being overwhelmed may be mostly perception, but it also could indicate problems in the program structure. For example, is the special educator trying to co-teach across content areas in a high school and not able to keep up with curriculum? Is an elementary special educator trying to keep traditional pullout services for all students while at the same time also trying to co-teach?

Addressing this problem requires finding its source and designing ways to address the core problems. A strategy as simple as having special education staff meet to discuss their experiences may help, as may having teachers visit successful co-teaching programs in nearby schools. Another possibility is doing a job analysis for the special educator to identify whether any services are being duplicated, whether some students might be receiving too much service (thereby causing problems in terms of workload for the special educator), or whether services could be re-arranged in order to streamline them.

I teach in the related arts (i.e., art, music, physical education, drama, media/technology). I work with nearly every student in school who has an IEP or who is an English language learner. However, I have no support at all, neither a co-teacher nor paraprofessional support. Shouldn't I be as entitled to some type of assistance just like all the other teachers?

Related arts classes as well as electives (for example, drama, web design) or non-core academic classes (for example, Spanish I, public speaking) seem to be short-changed when co-teaching is designed. A review of the support needs in such classes should occur right along with the analysis completed for core academic courses. If all students must take a keyboarding class, a decision to provide co-teaching in that class can be justified. However, professionals need to have direct conversations about priorities and resources. While it would be wonderful to have co-teaching available in every middle and high school course, this is not warranted, nor is it feasible. In some schools, paraprofessionals are assigned to such classes, at least on a part-time basis, so some assistance can be available even if daily fulltime support cannot be offered. A message that does not seem kind but that is nonetheless true is that students with disabilities are not entitled to support in every class taken, and for electives and non-core academic courses, no other option may exist.

Whether you work in an elementary, middle or high school, do be sure that all professionals, including those in the related arts and other courses, are part of conversations about how to design effective services for students with disabilities. By considering all participants' perspectives during program design and making sure the concerns of these valuable staff members are on the table along with those of the other educators, options for addressing them (even if they cannot be completely resolved) are more likely.

Questions and Concerns Related to Students, Parents, and the Delivery of Special Education Services

The trend to educate students with disabilities in general education settings in no way reduces the obligation of professionals to be sure students receive the special education and related services to which they are entitled. They also need to communicate with parents about this change in the expectations for students with disabilities and the implications for each child. These are some of the questions that may occur.

The students in the co-taught classroom are functioning several grade levels below other students, and their IEP goals and objectives reflect this. How is it possible to address these students' IEPs in the context of a fast-paced general education classroom where emphasis is on learning the grade level curriculum?

This question is understandable and reflects the collision between traditional thinking about special education and emerging contemporary practices. The first part of this issue raises the question about how IEPs are being written. For nearly all students with disabilities, the aim now is to base instruction in the grade level curriculum, even if the student's skills are assessed at a lower level. For example, if the sixth grade curriculum notes that students will be able to listen critically and offer their opinion orally, including stating fact and opinion, an IEP oral language goal should be written within this grade level expectation. That is, the student might carry out the grade level proficiency but do so having listened to a simpler passage. In today's schools, IEP goals should not exist in a vacuum; they must relate to grade level standards.

Another dimension to this question concerns providing necessary remediation for some students. For young students where the concern is reading and language arts skills, these needs should be addressed as part of the overall language arts program. That is, elementary programs should include a segment of time each day when students are grouped based on their assessed needs; during this time the most struggling readers would be together to receive intense instruction.

Another aspect of this question may relate to the level of student needs and the flexibility for meeting them. Professionals could decide that for a few students, an intense instructional arrangement in a separate setting is necessary. If this is the case, they should not think that this is not allowed, but they should gather detailed data to determine whether using this more restrictive instructional environment produces the intended results. If it does, it can be continued, but if it does not then it cannot be justified.

Delivering special education services in today's schools has become a complicated business. Clearly, students must receive their specialized instruction and related services. At the same time, services must be offered in the least restrictive environment, and the presumption in most cases is that the LRE is the general education classroom. Layered on these expectations are the mandates in current legislation that students have access to the general curriculum as it is taught by teachers highly qualified in the content areas. The task for professionals is to keep a healthy tension among all these factors so that students can reach their potential.

How should co-teaching be indicated on a student's IEP?

This question usually comes up when no state or local policy exists regarding this matter. If you are wondering about this topic, your first strategy should be to check with a special education administrator to see if guidelines for noting co-teaching are in place. In some states and districts, co-teaching is listed separately as the means through which a student will receive special education services. In others, co-teaching is written in as an option. In yet others, co-teaching is considered being educated in general education with direct service provided there. In a few locales, co-teaching is not noted on IEPs at all. Because so many policies exist regarding indicating co-teaching on IEPs, no single answer can be given. If you are unable to obtain a definitive answer locally, you should at least be consistent in how you (and colleagues who also are writing IEPs) specify that co-teaching is being provided.

What does co-teaching look like for students with significant intellectual disabilities? Should they be part of this model for providing special education services?

This question has no single answer, and it can only be discussed based on local policies and beliefs. Experience suggests that students with significant disabilities benefit greatly when they are part of a co-teaching program. This practice can help to meet the IDEA requirement that they receive their education in the least restrictive environment. In a few communities, students with significant intellectual disabilities may spend most of their school day in a classroom characterized by co-teaching and, possibly, paraprofessional support. This is most likely to occur at the elementary level. In most regions of the country, though, co-teaching for students with significant intellectual disabilities occurs on a part-time basis, often dependent on specific student need and staffing. The most common pattern is for these students to join a class already being co-taught by a teacher for students with learning disabilities or behavior disorders. By using this approach, the teacher in the separate class for students with significant disabilities can remain there while the students who participate in general education continue to receive special education support. An alternative is for a paraprofessional to accompany these students, offering support in the general education setting rather than co-teaching. Again, this strategy for co-teaching is most often seen at the elementary level.

This question is one that has many layers of implications. The high-stakes testing and accountability climate in today's schools has resulted, in some communities, in students with significant intellectual disabilities largely being excluded from participation in core general education content, usually justified on the fact that these students take an alternative assessment and cannot be allowed to "interfere" with the instruction that must be delivered to other students. In other schools, the notion of students with significant intellectual disabilities participating in co-teaching has not even been considered. If this is a concern in your school, it may be a topic that is appropriate for a careful and reflective discussion about inclusive practices and the service delivery options used in inclusive schools.

Does co-teaching work for students who are English language learners (ELLs)?

The majority of ideas and suggestions presented in this handbook are valid as program consideration for English language learners. This topic has been written about for a number of years (e.g., Bahamonde & Friend, 1999), but the trend toward delivery services to these learners in the general education setting has been slow to emerge and few data have been reported on its impact on student outcomes. Interest in this topic and programs that include co-teaching as a component are beginning to emerge, though. If you are interested in this specialized application of co-teaching, you are encouraged to stay alert to the professional literature that is beginning to address this topic (for example, Stoessel & Miles, n.d.).

Should inclusive practices and co-teaching also apply to programs for students who are gifted and talented?

This question probably has a large dollop of local policy and politics in it, and so any answer must be weighed against those local issues. In general, if students who are gifted and talented are thought of in the same way as all students, the answer becomes apparent. That is, just like for other students with exceptional needs, a few students who are gifted and talented have needs so special that they require separate services, at least part of the time. However, for many students, if they are grouped in classrooms (as was recommended for students with disabilities) and services are delivered to them in that setting, their needs are met and at the same time other students benefit as well (Tomlinson, Kaplan, Renzulli, Purcell, Leppien, & Bruns, 2002; Tomlinson, 2005).

Keep in mind that services for students who are gifted and talented are not mandated by federal legislation, and so the types of programs offered, the number of personnel available to deliver them, and the ways in which the program operate vary considerably from state to state and locale to locale. Professionals considering co-teaching as a service delivery model for students who are gifted and talented probably should explore this topic in the professional literature, outline goals of the planned program, establish criteria for determining its success, implement it gradually, and evaluate its impact on students.

I was surprised when several parents of students with disabilities told me they did not want their children in co-taught classes; they want instruction in the separate setting to be continued. Does this mean that we shouldn't co-teach?

A decision about the educational environment most appropriate for a student with a disability is made by the team that writes the IEP, not by the teachers, other professionals alone, or individual parents. Placement must be based on the assessed needs of the student, the type of instruction needed, and the supplementary aids and services that can be provided to support the student in a general education setting.

If a parent is concerned about a co-taught class, you should ask what the concern is. Some parents like the idea of a small, highly structured class and value the protection of their children over the growing expectations (and related pressure and stress) for achieving higher standards. Parents of students in high school—students who may for most of their education have been in separate setting for core academic instruction—may truly question whether their children can be educated there. For the first group of parents, it might be possible to suggest an IEP be implemented for a defined period of time (such as a grading period) and then reviewed. For the latter group of parents, the reluctance is understandable and it may not be appropriate to make a dramatic shift in services during a student's final year or two of school.

Professionals' responsibility to all parents of students with disabilities is to listen carefully to their concerns, ask questions to obtain a fuller understanding, and then try to work with parents to find a solution. Co-teaching often is a way to provide special education services in the least restrictive environment, but it is not the only option that should exist (and it cannot be the only service available to students regardless of their needs). Each student's situation must be considered individually by the IEP team and decisions reached based on the student's assessed needs and goals written.

The parents of one of the students in our class, a student who is an average learner, have complained to our principal that they do not want their child in co-teaching and will go to the school board if he is not moved to another class. Is a parent allowed to make this type of demand?

Most parents of typical learners are either unaware of the co-teaching program in their children's school, or they are strongly supportive of the benefits of co-teaching their children derive. When parents express concerns, professionals first must try to understand the basis for them. Just as with parents of students with disabilities listening is the beginning point. Some parents may have a vague concern that the students with disabilities will somehow cause the instruction to be watered down or standards to be lowered. This concern can easily be laid to rest. Other parents may object to their children being educated with the students they refer to as "those kids." What they may not realize is that their children have always been in classes with students with disabilities; co-teaching programs and bringing special education services into the general education usually is the only change occurring, not the membership of the class.

Administrators and teachers should be respectful of parent perspectives and attempt to address concerns, but acquiescing to parents' requests to place their children in particular classrooms and not in others can lead to a sort of contagion of rejection. The direct answer to this question is that public schools are just that—public schools—and parents do not have the option of deciding which children should be their children's classmates. This is a matter for principals to address; they often ask parents to describe their children's characteristics and then gently inform them that the final decision about which classroom is one that school professionals, not parents, make. One principal learned this lesson the hard way: In the first year of co-teaching he invited parents to volunteer their children for the co-taught classes, and no one volunteered. He was placed in the position of making decisions that were perceived by parents as broken promises. The next year (and every year since then), he adopted a policy of creating class groups based on input from teachers and parents, but with his final decision. What could have remained a significant source of conflict is now seldom mentioned.

One final comment on this topic should be made. Occasionally, parents will voice a legitimate concern about their child's placement. If a student with a disability has been physically aggressive with their child or if their child has been repeatedly asked to assist a child with a disability, their concerns should be addressed. Overall, though, this problem occurs only occasionally and usually can be solved with clear policies and respectful communication.

For Further Thought

1. Many of the topics addressed in this chapter that relate to the professional partnership could be prevented or quickly resolved through effective communication and the building of collaboration. Why do you think it is still difficult in many schools for professionals to speak with each other directly about issues related to their partnership? Do you think this varies by school level—elementary, middle, or high? Years of experience of the professionals co-teaching? On what experiences or readings are your opinions based?

2. As you review the topics in the section on program structure and logistics, consider how each (or a variation of each) pertains to your school. How are you addressing these topics? Why is administrative support so essential in addressing nearly every issue that was raised?

3. What steps would you suggest taking in a school just introducing co-teaching as a means of avoiding concerns raised by both parents of students with disabilities and parents of typical learners? Which strategies might work at elementary, middle and high school? Which might suit one level of school more than another?

Taking Action

1. Using the issues raised in this chapter and others that may be concerns in your school, create a brief survey to distribute to staff members. Use the information you gather to make recommendations about refining your co-teaching program.

2. With a committee or task force, discuss issues that have arisen or may arise regarding co-teaching services. Then identify ways to directly address them. For those anticipated, identify and implement proactive strategies for sharing information that could prevent them from ever becoming a concern.

3. If your school has several concerns regarding co-teaching, see if it would be possible for several professionals to visit a school that has addressed similar matters. It is suggested that a set of goals be identified for this visit and questions be prepared to ask teachers and administrators at the school. After the visit, professionals should meet to ensure that the information they obtained as part of the visit is applied to the situation at their school.

References

Bahamonde, C., & Friend, M. (1999). Teaching English language learners: A proposal for effective service delivery through collaboration and co-teaching. *Journal of Educational and Psychological Consultation, 10,* 1–24.

Stoessel, S., & Miles, J. A. (n.d.). Co-teaching benefits mainstream and ESL children. *Curricululinks, 2*(1), 1, 3.

Tomlinson, C. A. (2005). Quality curriculum and instruction for highly able students. *Theory into Practice, 44,* 160-166.

Tomlinson, C. A., Kaplan, S. N., Renzulli, J. S., Purcell, J., Leppien, J., & Burns, D. (2002). *The parallel curriculum: A design to develop high potential and challenge high-ability learners.* St. Paul, MN: National Association for Gifted Children.

Walther-Thomas, C. S. (1997). Co-teaching experiences: The benefits and problems that teachers and principals report over time. *Journal of Learning Disabilities, 30,* 395–407.

NOTES

• • • • • •

NOTES

• • • • • •

NOTES

• • • • • •

NOTES

About The Author

Marilyn Friend, Ph.D., has spent her career as a general education teacher, special education teacher, teacher educator, and staff developer. She is currently Professor of Education in the Department of Specialized Education Services at the University of North Carolina at Greensboro where she teaches coursework on inclusive practices and collaboration among service providers. She has consulted with school professionals nationally and internationally and has made more than 1500 presentations in the United States, Canada, Europe, and Asia. Her goal is to facilitate professionals' collaboration on behalf of their students, assisting them to form productive and efficient work teams, make the most of co-teaching, learn the best ways to manage awkward or adversarial conversations, and communicate effectively with parents.

Other Materials and Books by Marilyn Friend

From the Forum on Education
Available at www.forumoneducation.org

The Power of Two: Including Students through Co-Teaching (2nd edition) (2004)
[videotape]. Bloomington, IN: Elephant Rock Productions. Co-produced with
Leonard Burrello and Jotham Burrello.

***Leading a District to Scale: Access to the General Education Curriculum for
Every Student*** (2001) [videotape]. Bloomington, IN: Elephant Rock Productions.
Co-produced with Leonard Burrello and Jotham Burrello.

Successful High School Inclusion: Making Access a Reality for All Students
(2001) [videotape]. Bloomington, IN: Elephant Rock Productions. Co-produced with
Leonard Burrello and Jotham Burrello.

Complexities of Collaboration (2000) [videotape]. Bloomington, IN: Elephant Rock
Productions. Co-produced with Leonard Burrello and Jotham Burrello.

From Allyn & Bacon

Available from a traditional bookstore or an electronic bookseller such as Amazon.com.

Friend, M. & Cook, L. (2007) ***Interactions: Collaboration skills for school professionals*** (5th edition). Boston: Allyn & Bacon.

Friend, M. & Bursuck, W. (2009). ***Including Students with special needs: A practical guide for classroom teachers*** (5th edition). Boston: Allyn & Bacon.

Friend, M. (2008). ***Special education: Contemporary Perspectives for school professionals*** (2nd edition). Boston: Allyn & Bacon.